A NEW BANANA

*Unpeel YourSelf
and Elevate Your
Relationships*

Alessandra Veronesi

HOLY SHIVER

DISCLAIMER:

Every word in this book has been written with love and intention to help guide readers on the journey to inner peace and lifetime bliss. These are, in fact, opinions and suggestions. Not to be accepted as truth, unless they resonate…in which case, they were already your opinion, too!

A New Banana
© 2023; Alessandra Veronesi (Holy Shiver)

All rights reserved. If this material is wished to be used elsewhere, please ask the copyright owner. Text may only be reproduced with written permission.

It is illegal to copy this book, post it to a website, or distribute it by any other means without permission.

ISBN: 979-12-210-3351-9

First Edition

ACKNOWLEDGEMENTS

In no particular order, and not exhaustively, I'd like to thank all the circumstances and fellow human beings I've encountered along my path, including:

- The gentleman at the post office who traded me his ticket because I was in a rush. Thank you for showing me the kindness of a stranger.

- The people who do their best working a government job, keeping a smile despite the frustrating moments.

- The woman at the airport who gave me a break and did not charge me for rebooking.

- My colleagues and superiors, who remembered my value.

- The customer service representatives who make a difference.

- My friends, who have been there during moments in which I couldn't be there for myself, for exemplifying non-judgment and infinite laughter.

- My teachers and mentors, who have taken the time to explain their points of view.

- My parents for giving me life and loving me for who I am.

- Myself, for understanding how to turn this puzzle of life into one of the most beautiful mosaics I could have ever envisioned.

- You, and all the people who trusted me to show them how to heal themselves. Thank you for being a part of this journey.

To the good weather, the bad weather, the wise trees in the forest, the chirping birds, the buzzing bees, the fly that wouldn't find the window, the children who said I was beautiful, the exes who misunderstood me, the cheeses that made me fat and the salads that made me skinny. To the breeze of the sea, the waves crashing in the ocean, the sun on my skin and the fire in my heart.

To the socks that I lost and the habits that found me. To the spices in my food and the freshness of the perfect tomato.

To the massages that lasted longer and the lessons that ended early.

To my two dog children, Dolce and Holly, for teaching me the beauty of pure love and companionship, cuddles and kisses, and the privilege of responsibility. And later, when the cycle of life came to a close, for allowing me to experience and understand the most important journey of all.

To my dearest grandmothers: Jacqueline, who taught me science, biology, stock market investing, pragmatism, and French cooking; and Carmela, who showed me dedication, strength, and unconditional love, playing cards with me and showing me the secrets of making amazing homemade pasta.

To my friends who are family.

To sushi nights alone. And taco nights together.

To my father Gherardo, for being the greatest and fairest man I could ever look up to. To my mother Kathleen, for her love, her journey, and her artistic femininity. And their loyal, precious dogs Arty and Pixie.

Acknowledgements

To my sister Isabella, a caring mother and incredible Soul to share the family experience with, my brother-in-law Faouzi for his perseverance and values, and their beautiful sons Adam and Ayan, and their sweet dog Sunny.

To Envita Rose, for being the pure white light that guided my way into understanding the energies that have always been here to support us.

To Alex, for your love and light.

To Gianluigi, beyond this energetic plane.

To Ilenia, for treading the path of victory.

To Jacopo, for always keeping it Real.

To Chiara, for the Universe in your heart.

To Tommy, for your inspiration.

To Paolo, first supporter and igniter of this journey.

To Carmen Riot Smith, whose copy editing is a privilege and inspiration, to Steve Kuhn, for the great typesetting journey we embarked upon and to Peter Selgin, for making the cover of my dreams.

To our Earth, our home. To the Sun, our compass. To the Moon, reflecting new truths. To the Stars, on this magical map. To the Plants, for the infinite connection. To Tío, for awakening the experience. To Fredy, for the chance to learn from you. And to the Universe, for expanding the playground.

I am not thanking mosquitos.

CONTENTS

Preface 9
Introduction 13

PART 1:
RELATIONSHIP WITH SELF

1. The Illusion 17
2. The Crisis 31
3. The Solution 47

PART 2:
RELATIONSHIPS WITH OTHERS

4. Relating to Others 65

PART 3:
RELATIONSHIP WITH THE UNIVERSE

5. Universal Laws 101
6. Energy 107

PART 4:
ROMANTIC RELATIONSHIPS

7. Dating 139
8. Early Togetherness 169
9. Partnership 197

Conclusion: Marriage 215

PREFACE

This book sprouted from within as an innocent seed patiently asking to be watered while I was in the middle of a crisis. It's an active exploration of observations I've gathered over time, mixed with personal insights and flashes of Universal understanding. Remnants of battles I tried to fight, then learned to witness and overcome.

I am not especially enlightened nor am I free from the struggles of human existence. I wanted to write this book. And so I did, and here we are.

We are more similar than we are different. I just happened to feel a curiosity, a calling to investigate some of the themes that continued to come up in my life, and a need to relieve and understand my internal suffering. And when it worked, I couldn't resist sharing the answers that helped me — solutions that continue to come up as I notice others in similar struggles.

It's real talk from someone who is still living her own process too, and always will be. Consider it a pep talk of sorts, with quirky observations. In some cases, I can't take the full credit for the wisdom such observations provide, but perhaps we can say the answers came from a Source outside of myself. I still find it helpful to refer back to this text from time to time. After all, life is a repeating cycle of awareness and healing. You just get faster at it so that you can focus on bigger and different challenges.

My goal is to share the awareness that has helped me overcome the blocks of difficult moments. Moments that in and of themselves weren't uniquely more challenging than others, but that I experienced with high intensity because of the state I found myself in when they happened. Unnecessary suffering.

The stories that lead us to suffering are unique, but the solutions are Universal. Big or small, the impact that tribulations have on us are relative to how we feel when they happen.

Having a daily practice is important, particularly when we are going through a difficult period, but also for the whole life journey. Whether we are healing, releasing, understanding or simply grounding, a daily practice includes anything we do somewhat ritualistically to ensure we are aligned and balanced. It can be anything that brings us peace, such as meditating, morning routines, a fifteen-minute reading session in the bathroom, astrology, or the way we wind down in the evening. When we discover our own form of daily practice, we learn what it means to honor ourselves, be with ourselves, to step out of the thinking mind and seek clarity from within. We start to appreciate the experience of life, we welcome new beginnings, we feel joy and compassion and attract good opportunities.

I still experience my share of inconveniences. Things that in the past would have derailed me now just pass through me. Sometimes I eat chocolate for breakfast, and that's okay. I think. It is a familiar discomfort, but I am a witness to the pain, and the joy, not an actor in it.

Life is a perpetual journey, our healing is a process, and we will always be tested to show up, to overcome, to enjoy, to just be. Us and our curveballs. Loving every single one of them, even the annoying ones, and appreciating what they are here to show us.

How extraordinary would it be to transform anxieties and paranoias into moments of deep gratitude and insight? Not as rationalization and overthinking but as natural side effects of our own beautifully growing relationship with ourselves and the Universe?

These meditations and strategies are not related to any current events at whatever point in time you are reading this, although our healing and that of the world do happen simultaneously. In fact, I propose that they must.

I suggest reading each section in sequence if you would like to immerse yourself in the full journey. Each chapter is also a standalone, so feel free to pick whichever one resonates with you the most and start there. In fact, if you are at a point in life where you're seeking specific guidance on one of these topics, then of course, cherry pick! There's no wrong way to do it. Part one speaks on how to be human. Parts two and three teach us how to relate to others and build a beautiful relationship with our purpose and the Universe. And part four is, *oooh la la*, romantic!

But before we dive in, I'd like to explain my reasoning behind the structure of the book, as it is not by accident that these chapters fell in this order. Though this journey was closely tied to the desire to strengthen my relationship with the Universe, it began as an exploration to soothe my own suffering. So, in simpler terms, this first part covers our relationship with ourselves.

As Plato once said, *The beginning is the most important part of the work.*

We start by taking a look at ourselves. A good, hard, human look at ourselves, including my own story for an added touch of vulnerability.

We look at the entanglements and survival strategies we have adopted in order to get where we are today. We are the main characters in our own Book of Life and perpetual disciples of its lessons. This discipleship is the most important notion to be familiar with. Once we recognize the role of constant learning, we are no longer disappointed in the things we do, because we see their purpose is to teach us something. Without a true understanding of ourselves, we cannot expect to develop clarity in our pursuit of healthy dynamics with others and within our daily lives. This understanding is necessary to maintain and defend on an ongoing basis. The Universe is both inside of us and outside of us; we are microcosms of the macrocosm.

Next, we move on to applying the faith we have in ourselves to our daily lives, including in our friendships, work relationships, and interactions with strangers. We also cover some general guidelines for manifesting and cool ways we can make the most of our existence on this 3D plane.

Finally, we land back into the carnal pleasures of romantic relationships. Here we explore all the juicy details that happen when we are meeting a fellow Soul who tickles our fancy and ruffles our featherbottoms. It gets messy, and sexy, and jealousy, all at once. It's the pleasurable side of human existence! This comes last because, guess what? First we work on ourselves—and love ourselves so much that we attract the world and the love we want.

I hope this book will lead you to expose and connect at least a part of the puzzle pieces you need in order to be well on your way to building your most authentic life, while feeling good.

Come and experience this journey with me.

If you'd like to get in touch, you can go to www.holyshiver.com and hit Contact Us or follow me on Instagram (@holy_shiver).

INTRODUCTION

The title of this book is meant to get you to smile, because life is meant to be fun! Hilarious, in fact. And though we will not talk much about bananas in the book, I hope you will enjoy the reminder to laugh each time you pick it up.

But why a banana?

Genetic evidence suggests the earliest bananas first appeared in 8,000 BC in Southeast Asia. Back then, they were full of seeds, which made them difficult to enjoy. With a little help from farming, these wonderful things transformed into the seedless, delicious, and nutritious fruits we know today.

Indisputably, you've always been a banana since the day you were born. Your parents were bananas, and so were their parents, and this is the reality.

We each came here with our own lineage in different shapes and colors, but we are all, deep down, bananas. Capable of great transformation!

Happy bananas know who they are, free from the constricting vines that once held them. They delight in relating to others and themselves, while unhappy bananas struggle to feel good about their bananaess.

How do you become *A New Banana*? One that thinks, feels, and attracts GOOD things into their lives, and is unafraid to transform and live from a place of centered freedom within and without?

You start by peeling off the layers and making room for your true Self to manifest from the inside out.

If you want to become *A New Banana*, this book is for you.

Love,
Holy Shiver

PART 1

RELATIONSHIP WITH SELF

CHAPTER 1

THE ILLUSION

*Sometimes life saves you from what you want,
so that it can give you what you need.*
ANONYMOUS

We are quite resilient, we humans. Multifaceted, free-thinking, stupendous beings capable of achieving incredible things when we put our minds to it. We are so powerful that anything we want to create, whether it be to our benefit or to our detriment, can come true.

All things are born in thought before they become reality. Everything we do, whether consciously or subconsciously, comes down to the frequencies and vibrations we emit through our energetic fields and what we attract from them.

When we win a competition, score highly on an exam, get the dream job we wanted, or find the partnership of a lifetime, we can safely assume that something about what we did to achieve it worked. We may never be fully aware of the real reasons something worked out, because there's often a Greater Order. If we miss the boat on any such things, perhaps we wrongly blame ourselves without knowing the real reason why it didn't work out because, again, there's often a Greater Order.

Some of us might even allow other people's opinions of our actions to impact us further, skewing our vision of the truth with their own projections of what we could have done differently and what we should do next. Well intentioned people like parents, friends, colleagues, and partners, who have their own healing journeys to go on, can interfere with ours if we allow them. Even a microstatement can influence us if we are 50/50 about a decision and vulnerable to hearing someone else's opinion. Not knowing ourselves is what creates and perpetuates a state of illusion early on in our lives.

We want to be good citizens who follow cultural norms and the expectations of our close-knit groups, so we say, "Okay, I will take this job in dentistry because it is safe, and it's what my cousins and parents did," or "I will pursue this career so that I can make a down payment on a house, get a mortgage, and start a family." Even if, deep inside, we have a calling to do something else, we still believe others when they tell us it's too risky, that we could lose all our savings. So we choose the tried and true of safety and someone else's dream.

This is how we live in the Illusion. In the Illusion we are surrounded by others who are doing the same; certain difficulties become normalized—like sacrificing our self-expression and time, the guilt of not doing enough, and other concepts. When we live this way for a while it can be hard to pinpoint exactly what it is we are feeling, but at some point we sense that something is off.

Luckily, we need not know every piece of the puzzle or where they need to go before solving it. Any moment of dissatisfaction is excellent! To be treasured! Dissatisfaction, sadness, depression, anger, whatever that first puzzle piece may be, when we witness it, we can rearrange it and begin to see what it means to become ourselves. Piece by piece, we can choose how to get there.

Let's choose to wake up and claim happiness for ourselves! In being willing to question the mechanisms (internal and external) that have brought us here, we find the key that unlocks our peace in the moment and a blissful future in alignment with our life expression.

Let us not forget we are all connected. As we build ourselves authentically, we become strengthened by what makes us unique and supported in what makes us similar. And when we begin the journey of healing ourselves, we naturally extend this energy to others, simply by feeling good about who we are. Our frequency changes and the whole world around us opens up in our favor.

First we fix ourselves. First we learn how to quiet the mind. Then we make room for the magic growth. Then we begin to shine with wisdom and connection. Now life begins! Now life is fun! Now we are no one and someone, just like everybody else. Now the path is colorful and deliciously mysterious through a language we learn to decode every day.

Now loving comes easy, receiving is easy, hugging is the best, and following the arrow of our truth becomes clear.

I lived the Illusion for the first thirty-four years of my life. I was living the Illusion that everything was fine, as long as I could make it through another day, if only I succeeded in deluding myself and others that I was happy and successful. I would seek healing in various ways through conventional life coaching and therapy, internet research, or well-intentioned biased advice, but I was resonating with the frequencies of people who were also living the Illusion. I seemed like I was doing fine, even great. But it wasn't until I found the path to myself in a different way that I found the real answers and solutions. Then the true suffering of unawareness ended.

Every story begins differently, but the truths are Universal. So I invite you to read this flavor of one person's past that happens to be mine, and I hope you enjoy the story.

MY BANANA BEGINNING

Up until I was twelve years old I was sure I had been delivered by a magical gnome, during a Madonna concert outside the hospital window in the heart of Milan. Two of these statements are true. I later learned the doctor who delivered me was, in fact, only named Dr. Nomi, which is a phonetic stretch for 'gnome' and a testament to my mother's creativity.

Growth happened rather quickly, with the exception of my hair. I was a bald, adult baby, speaking, comprehending, and walking around with a disproportionately low number of follicles.

My birth name is Alessandra Veronesi. This is still my name. I chose to be born to a set of uniquely loving and wounded parents, an Italian executive and his artist wife. My father, a handsome bachelor in his days and excellent provider, and my mother, a beautiful former model from California who painted in Tuscany in the summers. They met in Paris. And for about ten years, we led an idyllic life in Italy.

Wafting from Italy to the US during various phases of childhood and adulthood, my greatest desire was for a less complicated life. I wanted something as simple as having family in the same country, and more than anything I wanted to stop having to make new friends, over and over and over.

Emotionally, the path wasn't always roses and daisies at our house, despite photographic evidence proving otherwise. And like many who end up in this dynamic, I became a very young marriage therapist for my parents.

When my dad lost his job, the lifestyle downgrade swept the proverbial rug from underneath our feet.

We lived in an affluent town in America, but in one of the smallest homes. My friends' basements were larger than our home. Not to say our home wasn't big, more to give an idea of the size of my friends' basements. My first boyfriend had a glass elevator and his very own living room attached to his bedroom. These are silly things in retrospect, but tell that to a teenager who is biologically programmed to compare herself to her peers. In my particular journey, this had a significant impact on the mask I chose to wear for the years to follow, including the career choices I would make and the decision to put financial security before my own freedom and Soul expression.

The Outer Layers

As I grew into post-college adulthood, it appeared on the outside that I had everything anyone could want. I followed the steps! A nice luxury apartment near New York City, a corporate job paying for my MBA, and a membership at a boutique pilates studio where no one was overweight. A lifestyle of $7 blended lavender almond-milk lattes, and non-ironically watching *The Bachelor* while drinking goblets of wine.

I remember walking to work one morning, going through the motions, feeling averagely content, when a construction worker said hello to me. I, in turn, put up my defenses and prepared to hear the standard catcall, as I so often did at twenty-six. Instead he said, "You have so much going for you. You see that, right? Be grateful." It wasn't menacing, it was kind. Matter-of-fact. I thanked him, but I remember thinking, *What is he saying? He has no idea how difficult it is to be happy. If only he knew how I feel inside. I don't even know how I feel inside. Good for him that he sees this. This is all a facade.*

We were both right.

Each day I would clock into work and proceed with my processes, documents, and meetings and later clock out, go to the gym, head home, open a bottle of wine, order takeout, and watch Netflix. Sometimes a little voice would enter and say, *What are we doing? Who are we helping?* Nada. All I saw was my own healthy paycheck coming in, and a lot of people perfectly satisfied to be there, in exchange for security. I strived to imitate their vibe and find fulfillment in getting my ducks in a row. It was comfortable, I won't lie. Though I *was* lying to myself.

The weekends were filled with brunches, slow-drip coffee, a walk on the waterfront, going out to the bars or enjoying a nice joint at home to escape temporarily. How I loved the escape. But there was a huge void inside of me. The void of not feeling alive. Of going through the motions. Laughing with friends about how the "struggle" was real. The struggle meaning "Not enough vacation days to escape to Mexico," "Not being able to handle your hangovers the way you used to in college," and "When your boss actually expects you to work."

Perhaps your version of outer layers looks different than mine. My story is just my story. One of many stories that lead to someone finding themselves. I was going through the motions without questioning the big picture. I was spinning on the hamster wheel for a lifestyle I could only enjoy on weekends, spending money to be happy but not really enjoying it since I was not fulfilled in myself to begin with.

The Big Move

Growing up biculturally, with half of my life in Europe and half of my life in the United States, I was quite conflicted over where to reside and who I was. I played around with the idea of moving back to Europe many times, but of course I had my ducks in a row in New York and a pilates studio where nobody was out of shape. Big conundrum.

Eventually, though, I grew tired of hearing myself talk about the same thing. So, little by little, I got moving. I decided to let my boss know this was my plan, and he supported me. The president of my company also generously supported me, stating that he would help me with introductions once I settled in my new city.

After completing my MBA, I hired a therapist for the last six weeks to mentally get me in gear, and I booked a one-way ticket to Italy in August of 2017. I had no job, some savings, and even less self-awareness. But the move invigorated me and I learned many things about Italy that I hadn't known before.

Like how uncomfortable the average couch was. That the water pressure is not so prioritized in a bathroom setting. And that all Chinese restaurants (in Italy) have conspired to *not* serve side sauce with their dumplings. But, I had done it! I had arrived.

It was time to prove myself. An uncertain time, but a heroic time of sorts. It meant waking up in the middle of the night terrified, wondering what I'd done with my life. Had I just committed career suicide? How would I pick myself back up if this flopped? How could I get myself a seat in a company and dial back into a fast track to success?

I was asleep still, but life was starting to wake me up with its discomforts.

I was also in a relationship.

The Shedding of the First Peel

This is my story, and in my story, my inability to fully choose (i.e. love) myself at the time of this relationship hindered its growth and, even more likely, unnecessarily perpetuated its length, as there were many signs I refused to face (though I will spare you the details). Maybe in your story, you and your partner are able to heal together! This is also very possible and true.

But to use the ever so eloquent legal terminology, we had irreconcilable differences. I would sit in meetings in London Mayfair surrounded by expensive artwork, listening to hundreds of millions of euros flying around like it was just another Tuesday. Because it was. And on the weekends, I would return to simplicity, and mushroom picking, and chestnuts in the mountains. On a weekly basis for almost two years, I'd switch from diamond-studded tennis bracelets to someone's uncle's gardening gloves in a matter of days. I liked being both these people, and he preferred mainly the latter.

For better or worse, this realization was finalized only after I had downgraded to a lower-paying job in a little Italian town near him. A part of Italy where the economy is based on industrial trades such as tile-making, foam-mattress manufacturing, fruit slicing machines, and parmesan cheese factories. My new job was stable, and we lived in a little apartment with a cute rent (my share of the rent equaling the amount I paid in utilities when I was in New York). Life was quaint and dandy, though the couch was still uncomfortable. But I wanted to build something together, because if we were to live in a place with one taxi and two sushi restaurants, where the greatest attraction was a Decathlon, the only way I could justify it was to start a family.

He did not want to do so. His was a No that saw no chance of a Yes for at least ten years. So with tears, and hugs, and dealing with the cruelty of saying goodbye to a Soul your Soul cares for so deeply beyond the material, we said goodbye.

The Breakdown

Following the breakup, I was all out of sorts for about a day. My Soul, quite possibly, had temporarily left my body and I did not know up from down. The very next morning, though, I woke up to the birds chirping and a mystical energy carrying me into a heavenly vibe of hope I can only attribute to the angels.

Life was full of possibilities again! I was going to move back to Milan and meet international people, start a new life of excitement and wonder, and rebuild my career.

But life had other plans for me. For you, too. For the World. Two months later, the global pandemic of COVID-19 hit.

It hit us all in the ways we needed it to. Each of us received exactly what we needed in some extreme form. Some abruptly found themselves in a full house, kids screaming, spouses yearning for their spaces, chaos. Relationships ended, others started. Lovers could no longer see each other. And a sudden, intense fear washed over the globe, bringing us all together through web conferencing.

I, on the other hand, found myself utterly alone. Stuck in my apartment, in a tiny Italian town, without any human contact for weeks to come.

Twenty days into quarantine, I tried talking to myself in order to feel like I had company. I remember thinking how helpful it was in the moment! *What a great talk, Alessandra, you should do this more often.* A few minutes later, I'd find myself laughing hysterically at the notion this was happening. It was pure, delusional bliss!

As the laughter got louder, it led me to the realization that I was possibly going insane, and without any warning I began to cry. These were ugly tears, snotty and hiccupy. I was no longer sure that I wasn't going to do something silly. I felt completely desperate and alone. I needed to reach out, and that's when I called the police.

Since we couldn't leave our towns, I asked the police for a pass from both my current municipality and the one I was hoping to go to (where my family was, about an hour away). The police heard me and urged me to leave at once. But I suppose all I needed to hear was their approval to feel less trapped. I also met a friend that day on my walk to throw out the garbage, a twenty-one-year-old pizza delivery boy with whom I regularly ended up chatting at a distance. Those in-person conversations saved me.

So I stayed. Equipped with this new, alarming knowledge that a fine barrier separates us from insanity.

Holy Shiver was about to be born.

The Start of the Holy Shiver

> *To put the world in order, we must first put the nation in order; to put the nation in order, we must first put the family in order; to put the family in order, we must first cultivate our personal life; we must first set our hearts right.*
> **CONFUCIUS**

Instead of drinking lots of wine that night, as had become the approved coping method worldwide, I cleaned my house from top to bottom to some good music. I began working out regularly to YouTube videos, and more importantly, I discovered meditation. I didn't realize I was also adopting a meditative lifestyle in everything I did, but everything I did had its own little purpose. Cleaning the stove, reading a book, opening the window and watching the sky.

Each morning I would wake up to take a shower, melt back into bed with my two little dogs, and listen to Stephanie Canavesio's guided meditations. At 9 a.m. every day of the first few months of the pandemic, she would start an Instagram live at @presence_embodied and teach us to connect. She started my awakening—the feeling that *something was* finally working and it was *in* me.

I was still a mess but I was changing, because for one hour in my day I loved myself. I learned how to breathe and relax my heartbeat, and I understood what it meant to connect to mySelf. I started tuning into the awareness of being something greater than the name I was given, of who I might be in a state of deep and dreamless sleep.

More than anything, I was coming into contact with the notion that, all along, I'd had everything I needed to keep myself whole. Which was quite apropos, given the full lockdown situation we were in.

Holy Shiver was born as a joke. My friend and business friend Paolo came up with it at dinner, right before Covid hit. We had yet to experience the real benefits of meditation, and found the whole effort to be quite hilarious. It sounded like *Holy Sh*t* so the name fit the bill for some ironic meditations I had written. However, as life took me on my journey, I discovered a more pressing message. Meditation was working! I was healing and I wanted to share that with the world. Holy Shiver also refers to the chills and activations we feel during a spiritual moment of awakening. And that is the definition to keep in mind.

The road to internal peace is not a linear one. It's cyclical and intense. We take two steps forward and sometimes fall back seemingly further than where we started. Then we find a shortcut to solve a recurring issue and grow a little more, only to fall back again, this time with a little more awareness it's happening. We do this over and over, and learn to overcome so that the challenges are new. But this beautiful life provides us with an infinite number of challenges.

Until we find the key. The passe-partout that allows us to open the doors to the infinite challenges and see the beauty they hold within. Inside each one is the chance to discover new things about ourselves every time there's an up and every time there's a down.

CHAPTER 2

THE CRISIS

Don't let your struggle become your identity.
ANONYMOUS

When things aren't going smoothly. When you're not in flow. When you're SO not flowing you don't even recognize that you're not flowing. When everything sucks and you are feeling generally negative about yourself and your life direction…you could be experiencing a crisis.

A crisis can be a single moment of acute awareness where you freeze and experience panic about making a decision, or it can be a slow-burning state of existence during a particular phase in your life. In a crisis, you might not know who you are or what career path you want to invest in. You might fear that you are behind all your peers in self-actualization, and then freak out about *that*. There are many kinds of crises—financial, spiritual, romantic, sexual preference, midlife—but this particular section concerns a crisis of identity, of choosing life direction.

WHO ARE YOU, REALLY?

Thoughts lead on to purposes; purposes go forth in action; actions form habits; habits decide character; and character fixes our destiny.
TYRON EDWARDS

For many years of my life, I remember hearing that dreaded question when I would ask others for advice. "What is it that *you* want?" And I would say, "That's not my question. What do I need to do here? I'm asking *you* for advice!" Then I would explain the complicated web I had woven myself into, each external constituent at play, only for them to reply, "But only you can know what you want." Enter total crisis mode.

It is a simple question when someone asks you what you want, but really what they're asking you is this: Who are you really? What is this decision saying about you? What is your purpose? And it can be terrifying to admit you do not know. Of course, it's when you stop caring and follow your truth that you have total freedom and your specific reactions become irrelevant.

The moments that lead you to taking these discovery steps are known as a crisis of identity. When you learn to step outside of yourself to see within yourself, the layers begin to peel off and you start to understand the complexity behind which parts belong to your real self and which ones were socially constructed into your making.

We'll get there!

Making Decisions

> *The possibilities are numerous once we decide to act and not react.*
> **GEORGE BERNARD SHAW**

The ability to make decisions for ourselves is one of the most crucial aspects of self-realization because it is in these small moments that we transform into who we are.

Allow me to abide by a popular assumption that every decision you make, whether consciously or not, makes up who you are. When your thoughts are clouded by who you think you need to be, everything you do from that Illusion is a mutated form of the truth. Maybe you suppressed emotional needs in the name of keeping the peace. Maybe you had to behave a certain way to receive love from a caretaker. Or maybe you were often left alone and nobody showed up for you, and you learned to survive by abandoning yourself every time you felt bad. Just like playing Telephone, but instead of playing with your friends, each whisper in the circle was a part of you that made one slightly-off decision after the other. By the time you get to the last part of yourself in the present, the message has gone completely skewed, therefore so has your ability to make the decision.

Let's use another analogy. Imagine you are in a jungle. Thick trees surround you with lots of vines connecting them. You want to cross the jungle just like everyone else, and the only way you see yourself getting to the other side is by grabbing onto the vines. You see others doing the same, so it must be the way.

You begin to grapple with one vine after the other without thinking about how your arms hurt. Complaining is normalized by the other vine movers, and you're just fixated on making it out alive. You move and make choices without stopping to ask yourself why. You see others are doing it, so you keep going. You keep going, but it is out of fear for survival and blindness to any alternative. When you don't know which vine to grab onto because none of it makes sense to you anymore, you ask someone else, and they tell you to just keep going, and so you keep going like this.

This is how it sometimes happens in life. Instead of taking each decision alone as it stands, in the present moment, and trusting ourselves to act in truth without fear or ambition of the outcome, we continue to clutch at every vine we can find, begging it to take us to the next vine, and the next one. Each vine is a decision that is influenced by an expectation someone has of you, as is the one after, and the one after that.

When you're caught in this cycle, you don't realize how liberating and possible it is to let go and jump. Fall into the flow of the beautiful water below and allow it to carry you to the other side while you save your energy and—why not?—enjoy it. But you must surrender to the unknown and trust that the Universe will have your back. Maybe you don't need to cross the jungle. Maybe your path was meant to lead somewhere else. You cannot see this unless you stop to question, feel into your heart, and assess the situation. This is not an easy task while you are holding onto a vine for dear life.

Sometimes the vine will snap and you will fall, and for a moment you might realize how much you were struggling, how much your arms hurt from holding onto a reality that wasn't sustainable. Many of us have moments like this, yet instead of embracing the fall, we use up all the energy we have to find our way back into "the swing" of things. The familiar struggle.

It might feel scary but this is precisely the moment to detach, to move closer to ourselves, and to discover what a delicious and nutritious banana we can become, once broken from the vine. Most of us are afraid to take the risk.

It's baffling that people are sad when they lose their jobs. Jobs that, in truth, made them radically unhappy and unable to choose for themselves. They feel twice destroyed by this. Their sense of self is intricately woven into the perception the role allowed them to have and instead of taking its loss as an opportunity to rediscover themselves, they spend all their energy worrying about finding another job just like that one. They should instead be celebrating! This is their chance to make a huge decision leading towards all the other decisions that will open them up to who they are. And if they get into the right, positive state of mind, they will attract an even better thing for themselves. The truth that is aligned with them.

Freedom From Expectation

Expectations were like fine pottery. The harder you held them, the more likely they were to crack.
BRANDON SANDERSON

Ever have one of those mornings where you dread the alarm clock and wish for evening to come? You have a big presentation, meetings, deadlines, groceries, dentist, the works. All this pressure has taken over your whole day and it hasn't even started yet! You have no control over your time and freedom, and neither does anybody else, it seems, so you accept it. You're sitting on the train of your morning commute that you somehow managed to board on time and suddenly it breaks down. You are forced to stop and think. How uncomfortable. Life is giving you a chance to let go of the vine for a moment. But instead of noticing this, you get more worked up; *now* how are you going to get everything done on time? You wonder how long it will be before you need to message your work that you will be late. Time passes, and you think, *All right, I will just open up my computer and work from here.* But the computer crashes. And your phone has no reception.

This is a beautiful moment! How amazing it is to clear the board like this! How silly do all your daily obligations feel now, in retrospect? You look out the window and can finally breathe. This is the moment, and you are in it. This is how every moment should feel. Neutral, present, and free. You are enough, whether those things happen or not. Looking back, how easy might it have been to reschedule the dentist, take the afternoon off, ask your spouse to get the groceries, or simply order them online?

These extenuating circumstances don't happen every day, and if we do not actively seek them, moments like this can be few and far between. It's up to us to defend our time and be kind to ourselves when no one else will be.

Not Attached to a Path

> *Anything is one of a million paths. Therefore you must always keep in mind that a path is only a path; if you feel you should not follow it, you must not stay with it under any conditions.... But your decision to keep on the path or to leave it must be free of fear or ambition.*
>
> **CARLOS CASTANEDA**

The courage to act with our hearts rather than in fear is one of the most important lessons we need to learn in order to empower ourselves to lead a satisfying life. When you can act courageously, despite yearning for a desired outcome, you minimize all your suffering. Things just become things, a path is only a path, and options are simply options, there to help us move between plans. It's truth. Happiness is a byproduct of knowing this; it's an acceptance that life is out there doing its thing, and we are okay throughout it. Whether there are storms or happy days, we are okay.

Imagine not caring about anything that happens to you, including negative things, because you know that no matter what, things will work out in your favor. What does "in your favor" mean? It can mean you fell for someone who struggled to love themselves and it didn't work out, so you avoided being with a person who would have mistreated you. It can mean not getting that high-paying job you wanted, where the stress would have been crippling. It's essentially dodging bullets, or, depending on how you look at it, taking a bullet to the leg so you can avoid the one coming at your head.

Acting with our heart does not mean being in love with what we are going to do next, or feeling a strong emotion for what will be if we do not do something. In fact, acting with our heart should bring about the opposite: being equally non-attached to any given outcome, to hearing a yes or a no, and simply going with the natural flow of the energy.

The moment you act with your heart is the moment you can finally choose freely. Because no matter what happens, the Universe will have your back. All you need to do is find the space within you that tells you what you are seeking next, and then you do it. You do it without looking back and without looking forward. You stay in the moment; you stay in every moment that happens around you.

When you live in the past, even in a happy memory, and you try to relish it, you are preventing yourself from experiencing the joy of now. Worse, when you can't change a scenario but repeatedly play it over and over again in your mind in attempt to do so, you are bringing yourself into a state of regret, which does not bode well with the laws of the Universe (attraction).

When you live in the future—whether you are dreading the day you need to do something big, like perform on stage, or whether you are looking forward to something, like a vacation—you are setting yourself up for an expectation which may or may not happen, and therefore, possible disappointment.

So live in the now. Enjoy the day before your big presentation and live it peacefully. If something doesn't work out in your favor, that's great! How interesting that this minor inconvenience happened, and no big deal. You did your best in the moment and now you have learned.

And also! What if it goes well? See what life brings you in the pureness of the next moment brought on by your expectation-free decision. And when something does work out, because it will, that's great too! How interesting that it went surprisingly well. Don't get attached. What will be next?

Life is a mystery blend of fate and free will. Certain things may be meant to happen, but we have free will always. This applies to others as well as to ourselves. When we give others the gift of not expecting, we get to experience the spontaneous joy of free will together.

It's vital to keep doing what it is you want to do (without hurting others, of course). Remember: to practice making decisions unattached to the outcome is to follow your purpose.

CHOOSING PURPOSE

He who has a why can endure any how.
FRIEDRICH NIETZSCHE

Everything around you has a purpose, so why shouldn't you? It's a very important purpose; you wouldn't be here if you didn't have one. Finding purpose is easy for some, but if you are torn on this front, know that it is perfectly normal and good for this to be your story today.

I recently heard the story of a woman, a very noble and intelligent woman who is now retired. Picture slightly different times, in a small town in Italy. This wonderful woman graced the late sixties to late nineties with her work ethic and contributions. She was an accountant at the same company her entire lifetime. Though she was offered many opportunities to switch into banking, she later told her daughter, "I never left because I felt it would dishonor the person who recommended me for my first job." She felt a sense of duty and obligation to remain there for, oh, you know, just about her entire life! Of course, all the while feeling no passion for her considerably respectable job. Perhaps she wouldn't have felt any for banking either, but as a numbers person, who is to say? She chose not to risk it. She blocked the possibility of change and purpose based on societal expectations disguised as honor.

I used to believe I was broken. I didn't have a clear indication of what I wanted to do with my life or who I was. Fire knows its purpose, doctors know their purpose, artists manifest their purpose. What does an in-betweener like me have to offer the world? Dinner party conversation and great email etiquette? I felt trapped by my self-imposed limitations and fearfully chose a corporate career that would give me the material benefits I thought I needed. My decisions were skewed because even though I was acting in my purpose at times, I couldn't see myself acting in my purpose. I couldn't see mySelf. For example, I certainly knew being a product manager was not my purpose, but I didn't realize that I was acting in my purpose when I was motivating the developers at our morning meetings, uplifting them and cheering them on to succeed.

The truth is, finding your purpose is the most amazing thing that can happen to you. And it comes from finding yourSelf, in the big and small decisions, and aligning yourself with your most authentic, capital-S "Self."

What Do You Get Lost In?

> *Your purpose naturally is as unclear as your divine nature. To discover your purpose, you must reintroduce yourself to your divine nature. When you do, you'll begin to hear silent whispers directing you to your purpose.*
>
> **VAL UCHENDU**

In the beginning, when life starts to awaken within you, the voice of truth is faint and jumbled with a lot of other thoughts. We still have blocks that prevent us from fully understanding that a moment of enjoyment and pure bliss is our Soul speaking through us.

Life is meant to be enjoyable. Most of us need to claim this in order to make it happen. When we enjoy life, it's because we've found wholeness within, and that is when the voice of truth begins to speak louder.

Our purpose is anything that allows us to feel lost in our present moment. The things we cannot help doing in order to be happy.

Some of these things have a value in themselves, although they may not be monetizable. What's important is to recognize the things that bring us into a state of flow, ease, and oneness with the Universe and ourselves while we are doing them, and do more of them.

Examples might be reading a book, walking through nature, or painting. This doesn't necessarily mean we should quit our jobs to become editors, park rangers, and artists. But it could!

When you begin to recognize the feeling of getting lost in the things you like to do while in a full state of awareness (not high or drunk, to put it bluntly), your mind will gently press you for more. These are the kinds of *cravings* worth seeking.

It doesn't matter if you still feel clueless about your purpose, you will be at peace with life in the meantime (which *is* the purpose!) and you will remember once again what it means to be whole. The more you do that Soul-filling thing, the more it will find you. The people who enjoy similar cravings will find you too. And more importantly, you will find yourself. Trust that you will find yourself and you will.

When we don't know our purpose it's like missing a key. A key we didn't particularly notice or that over time we forgot we even owned. It was there in a pile and we never even bothered to check what door it opened. Now, years have passed and we've gone about our lives without even thinking about it. But it's there, patiently waiting for us. Until we remember we have the key, until we recognize its existence, there is no way we will ever find it. We must remember and then choose to find it. The answer to where it is lies in the satisfaction of the moment, so that is where we must go and get to know ourselves. And when we find our missing key, it will open all of the best doors for us.

All Can Play, All Can Win

> *There is no competition in destiny, each one has its own splendor.*
> **GOUTHAM**

Beyond your conscious awareness is a great plan that you took part in assembling. That plan is ever present, there in the background to assist you when you call upon it. Trust in the Wisdom of the Universe and the unresolved questions. Know there is a way for everyone to manifest their beautiful purpose and, contrary to our linear way of thinking, life is not a zero-sum game – three plus three can equal more than six. Eradicate all thoughts of envy or comparison now; it's just wasted energy and we have no time to go there. The world needs healing, and healing starts from each and every one of us figuring out what we need to do to help. Sometimes that means we are healers too, but at the very least it means we must create something with ourselves.

Just because your uncle's brother-in-law won the lottery, or your best friend founded a startup, or Angela Merkel's niece got a pony for her birthday, that does not mean the miracle of abundance ends there and that you remain out of luck. You are just as entitled to access your own abundance—not despite, not in spite of, just in general. One thousand percent your own abundance is there for you, and it's your own unique manifestation that unlocks your lock. Follow your flow, be in the moment, and stay in that space as long as you can, because that is where you access the fountain of resources that deliver your success.

Adidas and Puma were founded by two brothers who fought and ended up creating their own two amazing shoe empires. Tinder and

Bumble were separately founded by a former couple that split up (not so amicably, I am told). Plenty of parallel abundance blossomed regardless of the successful paths of other people. Take Lyft and Uber, Pepsi and Coke, Google Maps and Waze. And if we remove all correlations, where countless orange juice brands, cashew nuts, black teas and hot sauces can all make it, then truly we live in a world of abundance!

So do not concern yourself—at least, not with a negative perspective—with what others are doing. Be curious to the extent that you can be happy for others' successes, and, by all means, dedicate the attention and support you feel is worthwhile towards their endeavors. But spend your time pursuing your truth, discovering it daily, expanding on your present moment, and doing what feels right to you. The right people will resonate with and flock to your frequency, just as you do towards those of others, and your own castle of success will begin to build itself around you. Piece by piece, day by day, brick by brick.

When you realize there is not a moment to waste, there truly is not a moment to waste.

Finding Your Key

> *The two most important days in life are the day you were born and the day you find out why.*
> **MARK TWAIN**

We have phases in our lives where we reach awakening, and the first one is experiencing discomfort, the discomfort of knowing and experiencing there is more to life than what we've been told. Once we recognize the discomfort, we may seek comfort in solitude. It's normal to want to be alone to reflect and to protect ourselves from people who go against our Universal awakening. We are realigning ourselves with the Universe and its intentions for us.

Once we get past this phase of discomfort and isolation, we cross into a phase of rebirth. Through rebirth we begin to learn what truly makes us who we are. We seek situations that bring us closer to our authenticity. In this phase, our lives grow and manifest into what we truly want, and we become the person we envision. We can see and choose to be surrounded by what's right for us, including new people. After rebirth, we reach a new state of awareness where everything is more aligned with our true purpose and meaning in this world.

Rinse and repeat. To varying degrees. Forever.

Let's start by acknowledging this: The idea that you will have found your key by the end of this section is ambitious at best, but we are planting the seed of purpose and intention.

And just like when we plant a new seed in our garden, there are many components necessary for the garden to thrive. We must plant this seed of purpose early so that we may also recognize its beautiful flower when it blooms.

As we plant this garden together, understanding the parts of the garden and how they work together will help us find our key.

A luscious garden is made with rich soil, oxygen, water, sunlight, seeds, and lots and lots of care. We need the space for this garden, of course, and that is where our exquisite bodies come in. Our body is the temple of our Soul, the space for the garden. The soil is our mind. If the soil is unhealthy, we cannot expect to grow any healthy flowers.

The oxygen is our Soul, ever present and ethereal. Water is our ever-flowing thoughts. Sunlight represents the tangible results we produce through the seeds we plant. The flowers and plants that blossom are all the parts we develop within to grow the garden of our lives!

We will be planting lots of seeds after this seed of purpose, which takes a bit of time to germinate. The seed of focus, the seed of self-reliance, the seed of love, and a lot of other good seeds all planted into our minds. We will begin to watch each of them sprout as we attend to our seeds with the life-giving water of our new thoughts and the results that manifest because of those thoughts.

We are all someone to someone in this world. You could be the catalyst for one person's realization, or the smiling stranger that brightened the day of someone who was about to jump off a bridge. Maybe you were meant to play a certain role for your kids to heal, or you may have chosen to take on a very unique mission to aid humanity. What is that mission you chose for yourself? All you must do is remember.

CHAPTER 3

THE SOLUTION

Knowing your own darkness is the best method for dealing with the darknesses of other people.
CARL JUNG

We hold the solutions within ourselves to overcome all of the issues and challenges that come our way.

Sometimes you have to keep reminding yourself of this, because you won't fully believe it. And other times you will feel it ignited within the depths of your own Soul's fire. You'll think, *That's it! Holy Moly, I am it! I am whole. I am the recipe. I am the food, and I am the mouth that eats it.*

But then you stumble, and that's so normal it's like breathing. And when you stumble, you might forget that burning fire because we are more wired to remember the negative than the positive. So if and when you do forget that moment, remember to be kind to yourself—because everyone, everyone, *everyone* has those days—and remember the actual solution: yourSelf. You are the solution. Say this truth to yourself even if you don't believe it. Say it until you do. Get used to saying it over and over and over again.

You will feel it, or perhaps you won't. It's okay. *Everything* is okay.

VULNERABILITY

Heroes are higher than their vulnerability, that is why they are heroes.
AMIT KALANTRI

It's good to be strong, but strength doesn't get enough credit and tends to be under-defined. Strength is more than the ability to withstand suffering or be able to lift heavy furniture. The highest form of strength is when we are able to open our hearts and share our most profound feelings, even fears, without laying them on another person to solve for us.

This form of strength is also called vulnerability.

Open Heart

Does this path have a heart? If it does, the path is good; if it doesn't, it is of no use. Both paths lead nowhere; but one has a heart, the other doesn't. One makes for a joyful journey; as long as you follow it, you are one with it. The other will make you curse your life.
CARLOS CASTANEDA

To be our own solution, we must take the path where the heart energy is most allied to our true course of action and not the path that the ego desires for fame or recognition, or the path of pleasing someone else's ego. When we reach the point where we are able to choose the path of our truth, we are then in a state of open heart. Having an open heart simply means that a yes is just as okay as a no. An open heart allows for things to flow and appear in alignment as you walk your path.

It takes courage to make open-hearted decisions, because we are essentially allowing ourselves to be naked, feeling what needs to be felt, acting on what needs to be done in order to continue moving into the direction of truth in our hearts.

Everyone's truth is different. If someone despises eggplant, even the best plate of baba ghanoush will not be the perfect dinner experience. We must have the courage to say no to a beautiful silver platter of baba ghanoush, and wait for the hummus or the fattoush salad to arrive.

Vulnerability means sharing the whole truth at the cost of opening ourselves up to reach that open heart. It means being in the moment of communication without needing to sway a situation into a particular outcome, because any outcome is perfectly allowed to manifest so long as we act purely. So long as we share our whole selves, open and strong. And when we feel this way—the more we feel this way—the more we can tap into authentically delivering messages. Manipulation is eradicated. Less and less we will look back on situations and think, *I should have said this! I should have mentioned that.* And even less will we wish to go back and change what has taken place. We will know the right time to share the messages that needed to reach us and be delivered through us. In communicating these messages, we will be carrying on our mission from the Universe.

We must not worry about why or how things are or are not happening. All we must do is simply act in the present moment, say what we need to say, be brave, and go for the truth at all times. Accepting the flow of life just as freely as we are giving it.

Transmit the information you fully feel without transferring your ego. Share your present and full self in the moment without fear or ambition.

Now, in the beginning this could feel strange. You might overshare, you might do something uncool, you might expose your most private interior to an audience that did not opt into it. That's okay! That is vulnerability on steroids, and *that* will prepare you to have compassion and accept it from others when they are also going through their process of opening up.

We as human beings, with veins and heartbeats and consciousnesses on this Earth, become pillars of truth for others once we recognize what it means, what it has done for us, and what it can do for others. Then we can heal the world. Then we can ripple-effect the real progress.

So you, my beautiful, as you are healing today, and continue to grow, will more and more often be placed in situations where you will have the chance to help others discover their greatness. And it will feel damn good to offer freedom of expression and acceptance of their vulnerability.

Honesty

> *The first step is to be honest, and then to be noble.*
> **WINSTON CHURCHILL**

In their simplest form, honesty, bravery, and kindness go together to make vulnerability. There are differences between them, but each can inspire sharing, exposing a hidden part of ourselves so the truth that needed to come out can manifest.

So what is the difference between plain honesty and vulnerability? Glad I asked. Let's spice things up with a sexual example that many of us may relate to from at least one side.

Imagine you've spent a considerable period of time (relative to each person's idea of time) getting to know someone, intensely respecting their intellect and learning their intricate eccentricities. Of course, during those twenty-four hours, or weeks, or months, you're sometimes wondering what they would feel like to you physically, because you're human. But you're really into them, mind-body-soul-*bam,* it's all there. Then you do it. You finally consecrate your attraction. You're nervous and excited and it's…well, less than stellar. It's fast, sudden, and highly successful for one of you. And in that classic post-coitus moment, the one who was quickly successful asks the one who was clearly not how it was.

"Was it good for you? Did you…?" Partner 1 asks.

And Partner 2 honestly replies, "Well, it felt good, but I didn't…"

And Partner 1, who really just has a thing for disliking themselves, will ask again, "What do you mean? It felt good, but you didn't…?"

And Partner 2 will think, *Oh God, I've ruined a fragile ego*, and will try to make it better, compliment the anatomy, and mumble something about trying again later. But it's too late because an aspect of insecurity perceives that everything being said is to make up for that moment with a tone of pity and consolation. Even the proposition of doing it again makes Partner 1 feel responsible to hold the pressure of that information.

"But that was honest," Partner 2 will say. *How generous I was to share this honesty*, they will think. *Isn't that the best, most right thing? Truth hurts*, Partner 2 will validate internally, silently making the pact that when they finally achieve orgasm Partner 1 will know and will authentically feel proud. Partner 2 thinks they are building a foundation of honesty and trust, but perhaps they are laying down a brick of distance between them.

What if instead Partner 2 had recognized their full truth, and said something like, "I didn't reach orgasm, because I really like you and being with you for the first time made me very nervous," then they has shared their vulnerability in courage, and Partner 1 will not feel responsible for their displeasure. Partner 2 has taken ownership of the problem and therefore the solution is less personal, more approachable.

Courage

> *Courage is vulnerability. Vulnerability is courage. Like shadow and light, neither one can exist without the other.*
> **WAI LAN YUEN**

We must work towards bridging the gap between the person we see ourselves to be, the person others see we are, and the person we wish to become. When those three aspects have become one, we are primed for vulnerability, as well as many other glorious things.

This takes courage. It takes courage to speak up and admit wrongdoing when others are praising you. It takes courage to be honorable when there is otherwise no reason to be. It takes courage to go into a public place and sing a tune out loud that others might enjoy.

And it takes courage for a little boy who has been excluded by his friends to walk up to them and let them know he feels hurt. In fact, perhaps ninety-nine out of one hundred times, that little boy will go home and not say anything and live his life with a tiny little chip on his shoulder for an inappropriately long amount of time. But, if he is aware of his pain later in life, if he can feel his pain just enough to remember it, then he can recognize this pattern in a new situation and begin to heal himself from there.

Courage means understanding that you have the ability to change everything you need to change right now, and actually doing it. Remember: you are the solution! You hold the key. And the beginning of change doesn't have to look like anything. It can be as simple as realizing that you are small and you have a long way to go. The first step is the silent pact you make with yourself, even now, that it is time to try a new road.

Do not listen to this nonsense of family patterns—you will not be just like your mom, or your cousin Ralph, or your great-aunt Eugenia. You are you, and if you have the awareness and understanding to preemptively investigate yourSelf, then I can assure you that you have everything you need to discover your truest Self, a Self unlike anyone you know in your family. It is you, your *you*-est you, before you were given a name, before you incarnated, before your awareness turned into physical consciousness.

Perhaps the final courage I will whisper for you to consider is the courage to love yourself. That too is vulnerable. As I write this, a little tear is fighting to come out. You are right there too, my dear, waiting for yourself to love you. And if there is one thing I wish for you, it's for you to discover this love for yourself over and over and over again in your life. It's the most important pillar for any act of courage and boundary setting that you will come across. You will need the courage to love yourself in order to keep your sanity in life and begin to create great things! So many great things can be created, like happiness, food, jobs, opportunities—so many great things.

As Brené Brown has stated, "Vulnerability is the birthplace of innovation, creativity and change." You have what it takes, I promise you. And if you don't know this, or you don't feel it, contact me via my website or Instagram. Make that an act of courage. We will talk.

POWER

One who knows himself is never disturbed
by what others think of him.
ANONYMOUS

I'm not talking about the kind of power that comes with repeated reinforcement. Real power is intangible and steady, ever-burning like a fire.

To be in your power, seek a clear understanding of the things available to you that bring you stability and flow. Both stability and flow are tools and strategies to ground you in the moment as well as in your long-term life practices and beliefs. Once you know these tools, you'll use them. When you use your strategies, you will see the progress you make in life, and you'll witness yourself inevitably improving without trying hard to be anything at all.

In the context of relationships, being in our power allows us to be unrattled by tangential things. It allows us to rise above any situation so that we may clearly and deliberately be our full, confident Self, reacting in truth and moving forward valiantly with our actions.

Knowing yourSelf allows you to recognize when you are in balance, and when you are out of balance. And recognizing when you are not feeling in balance is a step to being in your power in those moments as well.

To remain calm in every situation is peace, and when nothing disturbs you, you are in your power.

Nobody likes to stay up at night ruminating on the day's thoughts and behaviors, or what so-and-so thought of them, or what they should have done instead. This is torture.

Second-guessing yourself and focusing on the things you did wrong is an absurd waste of time, though it is a programming loop that our silly, ego-driven brains find deep comfort in.

We avoid this loop by knowing ourselves as fully as we can, programming warts and all. Step by step, as a disciple of life we start to see the person we are, were, and will be — which are all the same when we are in a state of awareness. As we establish a baseline of who we are in a variety of ever-evolving contexts, we learn to love ourselves, to recognize the team of angels (or any higher realms that resonate) supporting us, and we reach acceptance, and compassion, and faith.

Feeling worthy is absolutely key to power, as is humility.

Others can feel the power in us as long as we are comfortable with it within ourselves.

When someone else's stress doesn't affect us, and our calmness transmutes it, we are in our power. In the same way that when a rock is drowned in water, it enhances the mineral content of the water and remains a rock.

When we know how to take ourselves back into peace and safety, we are halfway to experiencing our power. Fixing ourselves settles the world around us. This can mean understanding when it is time to take a pause, meditate, reflect, distract ourselves with a physical activity. We must do this as many times as we feel necessary in the moments that trigger us.

Once we've mastered bringing ourselves back to peace, we will find it easier and easier to be at peace all the time so that we can be a beam of light and inspiration to others. And I promise you can get there.

In the background of your peace is the understanding that without Ego interference, Power is a responsibility to be humble in your greatness. Achieving success is a personal transformation where strength blesses you into power and freedom so that you may live in Purpose, carry forth your mission, and blossom into the manifestation of your true Self.

Peace Within

> *No man is free who is not master of himself*
> **EPICTETUS**

Imagine you are wrapped in an enchanted forest. The light seeps through the trees, just enough to sun-kiss your cheeks as you admire the intricate branching patterns gently undulating in the mid-morning breeze. You're sitting on the perfect rock, a little river streaming below you just enough to freshen the air even more. You are alone with your favorite book, and a little chipmunk pitter-patters towards you in adorable hesitation and decides it's safe to eat his hazelnuts beside you. One fills each cheek. You lock eyes while the birds chirp their symphony, and you're pretty sure there are fairies because sometimes you catch glimmering specks of stardust appearing in the trees.

Not everyone can sustainably access or remain in such a place. But this is one version of how inner peace could feel like inside of you.

What does it feel like in your happy place? Where do you go when you need to seek refuge within? When you have an idea of what that place feels like, it is always there for you, albeit distant at times.

You just need to learn how to bring it back. Life is a constant process of self-monitoring and self-regulating, but I promise you it's fun.

For example, let me invite you into my present. I am sitting in my childhood home which is about to be sold, attempting to work a pretty high-pressure job while an inspector is testing our carbon monoxide detector (inconsistent loud beeping for over an hour). There's a garage sale taking place outside that no one is monitoring and people are coming in and out of the house looking to negotiate down on our family treasures. I am also sitting on a half chair. A leather stool of sorts missing the top part of ergonomic comfort. It's not harmonious or ideal. It is, in fact, quite irritating as I work on relinquishing control, but I am here at peace. Or, attempting to be. Doing my best. Looking forward to laughing about it later.

Having a sense of peace, and even humor, within gives you the ability to stay calm. When things change inside of you, things change around you. And when you are calm, the whole Universe surrenders.

Freedom

> *Nothing should get in the way of your ability to choose freely.*
> **ENVITA ROSE HASLER**

Whether it be a relationship, drugs, alcohol, others' preconceived expectations, or fear of people's opinions of you, you should never feel pressured to act because of something or someone. When that feels like it's happening, remove yourself from the situation and ask what is truly driving your decision. When you act to appease others, you are ultimately manipulating them and the outcome of the situation. When you act to appease a habit of yours, you are perpetuating your own self-enslavement, not pursuing freedom.

People think manipulation is smart and conniving, but it's a trick we play on ourselves. When we attempt to control a miniscule outcome that someone else would otherwise execute freely, we're limited from exploring what we truly want. Allow everyone the same freedom you allow yourself—to make mistakes, to make progress, to make an impact.

Anything that gets in the way of choosing freely is something worth considering whether to eradicate or resolve. For example, if your desire to smoke a joint conditions you to choose staying in versus meeting great new people at an exciting event, then it might be worth recognizing the habit is preventing you from choosing freely and self-actualizing.

If your desire to act freely goes against your family's expectations and your family is controlling you with religion or inheritance, then it is worth checking internally whether you wish to give up your authentic self-expression in the name of approval or money. Family control can drive a lot of misplaced behaviors in us due to fear of disappointing or losing a support system.

Many of us also feel this familiar tug when we are at work. Very few are lucky enough to enjoy their jobs from a place of total fulfillment. The majority spend their whole lives preparing for the wrong job for the wrong reasons. We want to achieve future peace and freedom and often do so at the cost of our present peace and freedom. That's crazy! It's like paying ten dollars to have ten dollars. We work so hard to be "happy" that we are defeated and bitter. And we could end up resenting others for their easily achieved happiness, which is nonsense because happiness *is* easily achieved and should be celebrated.

True freedom is being light and free in our present. When someone asks whether you prefer an aisle seat or a window seat, how does that question feel? Easy choice, right? Simple, objective, and moderately self-disclosing. Each and every decision and outcome should not weigh down on you. When we are asked questions that feel heavy, perhaps there is a greater block behind those questions so they feel stickier to answer. We must resolve those blocks so the questions don't feel so heavy in the end.

For example, let's say someone asks you if they can borrow your car for the weekend. If you do not feel comfortable with that, it should be easy for you to say no. But perhaps you feel torn and unable to express your discomfort in the moment. Maybe you think to yourself, *A good person—a kind and generous person, the type of person I want to be—would say yes to this type of request.* And so you say yes out of obligation and not from your heart.

It's detrimental to fragment our beliefs with choices that aren't coming from our purest selves. It takes courage to discern and identify when to nip something in the bud, especially in a moment where someone has pushed our boundaries and made us feel uncomfortable. But that's where the key lies!

The key to Freedom lies in building a stronger and stronger relationship with your intuition through repeated experiences so that when these situations arise, a difficult question becomes just as easy to answer as an easy one. Every answer is a simple "yes," "no," or "I don't know." But the faster you can choose, the faster you move freely in life. Being able to move freely stems from the self-esteem of having discipline, knowing yourself in general, and checking in with yourself in the moments when you are caught unprepared. Freedom happens when we're not afraid to take some time to think things through. Freedom is being in charge of your own reactions, in your own time, with the calmness of knowing you know what is best. Understand this and you will easily and enjoyably navigate the rest.

The Self

> *Your visions will become clear only when you can look into your own heart. Who looks outside, dreams; who looks inside, awakens.*
> **CARL JUNG**

The Self. Quite the trickster, this one. Beware of self-delusion. Like a Sicilian fisherman trying to sell you extra calamari you don't need, the Self can sometimes over*sell* certain aspects of the decisions we make because it thinks taking that path will lead to great things.

And for a short period of time, we think we are making the absolute best decision. We easily reinforce it because we can find supportive evidence anywhere we look once we've chosen the direction we wish to take. This is how we remain stuck in ruts and cycles, how we lie to ourselves, and how we sometimes get caught in victim mindsets.

Look. We're all trying to feel good in life and optimize our chances at happiness. However, if we are choosing from a place of laziness or lack, then we need to be ready to face the consequences.

Getting to a place where you can feel centered and fulfilled within yourself takes preparation. To prepare, keep growing yourSelf and see how that feels. Do this by finding a way to enter a meditative state daily. You can do so through cooking, long walks in nature, driving long roads, or simply shutting your eyes and thinking about nothing.

The more you take the time to be alone, the more you develop a trust in yourSelf that allows you to recognize the subtle moments in your gut when something feels off. You will be able to get real with yourself, live with an open heart, and not be held back by lack of freedom in your choices.

The more you get to know and love yourSelf, the more you can identify and act from that Self.

Remember: As long as you are breathing, you can expect to work on yourself in life.

As Bob Dylan said once, "You always have to realize that you're constantly in a state of becoming. And as long as you stay in that realm, you'll sort of be alright."

Repeat what we learned earlier: you are the solution. Your relationship with Self, the life you live discovering it, is the glue that holds your life together. While you grow and learn, this is who will be beside you, cheering you on. To decide and discern, vouch for yourSelf and carry on authentic and direct relationships, expecting and inciting the same from others. You came into this world with your awareness and ultimately that is what you will leave with.

Listen to yourSelf and not your busy mind.

PART 2

RELATIONSHIPS WITH OTHERS

CHAPTER 4

RELATING TO OTHERS

Because true belonging only happens when we present our authentic, imperfect selves to the world, our sense of belonging can never be greater than our level of self-acceptance.
BRENÉ BROWN

Relating to others is simple and calm once you have embraced your own fullness of being. If you understand, accept, and learn how to put yourself into a state of wellness, the rest becomes easy. It becomes easy because how it shows up in the external doesn't matter! Honestly, it never mattered, but at least when you are aware of *how* you are, and confident in *who* you are, you'll have the added validation from yourself that anything you've done across a variety of social scenarios was fine and dandy.

For most human beings, life swings between situations where we feel inappropriate, appropriate, and perhaps overly cool. Each context teaches us a lesson, and the lesson at the root of it all is humility. Be humble when you feel struck down, be humble when everything is neutral and harmonious, and especially be humble when you feel *cooler* than the rest of the room. You're never cooler than anyone else, nor has anyone else been cooler than you—there's just alignment and unalignment. Someone doing or acting better than you (according to an objective standard that strikes a note for you) simply means they're less blocked, nothing more, nothing less. Learn from them, and don't be afraid to be vulnerable, unpretentious—admit you find them interesting, intriguing, inspiring.

Structures in our upbringing and early life experiences will impact how we come across and the courage we have to show up as our-Selves, unless we do the work to peel off the layers. Upon realizing this, a marvelous thing happens: We begin to accept ourselves along every stage of the way. We begin not to care, we begin to love ourselves no matter what, which allows us not to care about what we say or do "wrong." Situations simply exist as they may. We are free.

There's a difference between someone who says something strange and feels awkward about it and someone who admits it and laughs along with everyone at the table. As Nora Ephron once said, "When you slip on a banana peel, people laugh at you. But when you tell people you slipped on a banana peel, it's your laugh."

So, as we go into this chapter, recognize that you are the one writing the script. You choose how you want to feel at the beginning, middle, and end of any interaction. You can walk with your head held high and accept yourself first, setting the tone for others to do the same, or not. In all cases, be humble, and make room for others who have not yet accepted themselves.

When there is no judgment within, there is no judgment without. When you stop judging, you are less likely to attract judgment back. And if you do, it won't be on your radar. It will slide off you and back onto the other person. You'll be happy and content, smiling and mingling in a circle of great people, in the moment, rejoicing at the splendor of what's ahead.

STRANGERS

We sometimes encounter people, even perfect strangers, who begin to interest us at first sight, somehow suddenly, all at once, before a word has been spoken.

FYODOR DOSTOEVSKY

Your likelihood of meeting a true stranger is quite low. Our Souls have been around for millions if not billions of years, so it's more probable that your Soul has encountered most of the people you come across today in one lifetime and life form or another.

Most of us don't necessarily look at things this way in our daily lives, and that is completely okay as well because strangers, in their purest, most dictionary-friendly form, are the best! What's better than being able to be totally direct, in a moment, with no expectation but the interaction itself?

My favorite interactions on this planet are with strangers. Not that I don't love the people I am close with — there is just something unique and invigorating when you cross paths with a person you've never spoken to and may never speak with again. There are zero expectations. You can trade good vibes, and it's not even weird to be brusque upon exiting the scene. And if it is weird, who cares? You'll never see them again.

We must go over one thing — the Stranger-Stranger Conversation Law. Which I've just invented. The Stranger-Stranger Conversation Law states that within a Stranger-Stranger conversation, vibes supersede content. Words are nothing but a frock in which to dress your magical interaction.

We should never imprison our interlocutors, nor should they imprison us. A Stranger-Stranger conversation should be quick and low-pressure, without commitment or an expectation for follow-up. If they should come up, you kindly make this boundary known.

Consider this example:

> **Man:** *Yes, because when I was younger, I was thinking about so many others walking around thinking the world is flat without knowing it can be round. I remind people of this because it's absolutely vital for everyone to understand how these principles apply in their daily lives. Say you are going to the store and you want to buy bread. That bread is representative of something.*
>
> **You:** *Mmmhmmm.*
>
> **Man:** *So then I began studying the bread, and the ingredients, and I met other people who like to bake bread and mix ingredients. And there are a lot of people making bread in the world! You'd be surprised how the mechanism works, and how well organized it is.*
>
> **You:** *Great…*
>
> **Man:** *I think what matters most is understanding that when you spread jelly on your toast…(insert extended metaphor regarding jelly and toast)… because the toast and the jelly together enhance each other's flavors and when people's taste buds interact with the mix of the crunch, and the sweetness, and the…*
>
> **You:** *Perhaps we can all agree to the importance of bread and we must get going.*
>
> **Man:** *Thank you, you too!!! It was great to meet you as well!*

That's, at least, what the conversation felt like. I have not transcribed the extent of its lengthiness. Imagine a lot more jibber jabber. What was designed to be a two-minute *I appreciate you, you appreciate me* conversation became an unprompted, somewhat related conversation where I was no longer in control of my time to exit. This stranger violated the Stranger-Stranger Conversation Law of swiftness and imprisoned me in their narrative. But I reminded them of the interaction's purpose, and *voilà*…Presto pronto! Stranger interaction restored and complete!

Ideas on how you can boost the vibes of the day by being kind to a stranger:

- Let them know their tag is sticking out.

- Seriously compliment a man on their outfit, the way you would a woman (if you are a woman; if you are a man, compliment in the same way you see women complimenting women).

- Carry dog treats and give one to a homeless man's dog when you walk by.

- Let someone know they have a beautiful smile.

- Offer to take a photo for a family or a couple as you walk by.

- Wish someone a great day after holding the door open for them or they hold the door open for you.

- Tell someone they are simply beautiful.

Pressure-free interactions. Straight to the point with elements of kindness. No expectation of a response or committed engagement. No dangerously open-ended questions, just quick words and good vibes.

Oh, and if someone begins to rattle off on you in violation of the Stranger-Stranger Conversation Law, you are completely entitled to end the chat early and set a boundary! The good vibes will still come through.

Meeting New People

> *There are no strangers here:*
> *only friends you haven't yet met.*
> **WILLIAM BUTLER YEATS**

Meeting new people is a little bit more amplified than crossing paths with a stranger, since it involves a broader context or shared situation such as a dinner, destination wedding, or a spiritual retreat with like-minded individuals, etc.

These situations are more open-ended, which allows for deeper, more meaningful exchanges across a longer, yet still finite, stretch of time. There's a pre-established rapport thanks to the similarities that brought you into the situation to begin with. Conversations and experiences are facilitated — therefore, so is bonding.

When people meet new people, they seek similarities, thereby reducing uncertainty. What brought you into that situation is your launchpad. You start there, and if you like the person, you continue to build on that and find new ways to connect.

The key is simply to be in the moment. It's one of the best ways we can practice appreciation for the moment. This appreciation in and of itself makes space for the Universe to do its magic during the interaction — whatever that may bring. Perhaps you meet someone you can help further down the line with one of your connections, or you receive an introduction to an impactful person who is aligned with your path, or maybe you hear something from a new perspective, a casual anecdote that finally puts one of your mental anguishes to rest.

Destination weddings are one of my favorite times to meet new people because you are starting from a space of great love for the couple, in support of their union, and in celebration of life. At least one would hope this is the case, since the time and effort to be there act as a filter for this. At a destination wedding, it is understood that for at least a few days, you and (usually) less than thirty core people will be sharing meals, hotel space, cocktail parties, the wedding itself, and possibly a nice morning-after hangover brunch on a rooftop. So you inevitably merge! Great relationships can be formed as you relish the sights, take part in new discoveries, find new people to chat with at dinner. Ultimately, you return home with an experience that formed and enriched you. And like any similar experience, nobody will ever be able to take those moments away from you.

At the end of it, whether it's a simple dinner or a life-altering plant medicine retreat, the door is open as to whether or not that encounter will evolve into friendship or continued correspondence. In a way, in those moments, you did experience friendship—friendship in a capsule. And you will always have the experience, the footprints in your heart.

No expectations, of course—and if it ends there, that is perfect too.

No Expectations

> *Once I began to realize that there were no rules and that my path didn't have to look like everyone else's, I relaxed and my whole world opened up.*
>
> **G. BRIAN BENSON**

We touched upon the importance of no expectations at the end of the previous section. This guideline goes well with any of life's relationships. There's nothing worse than forcing a relationship because of our own expectations or the expectations others had for us. Having no expectations can also be positive! When we expect nothing, sweet surprises feel even sweeter. We must allow things to take their course, perfectly or imperfectly, and go with the flow, trusting there is wisdom in the golden string of life that unites us together. No tie can be severed among us on this earthly plane. We are all connected.

Allow me to entertain you with a radical concept.

Are you Me? Am I You?

What if the entire world as we know it — the land we have, the cities we've created, and all its people that we meet or hear about — are actually a perfectly and intricately created world we designed for ourselves to expand our own consciousness and awareness? A massive playground of perspective for us to learn in? What if *You*, reading this book, are still *Me* experiencing a different side of *My* experience? Or what if *I*, writing this book, am *You* experiencing a different side of *Your* experience? We'd be one and the same.

Wouldn't that change the way you treated and saw others? How would you react to someone lashing out in pain, someone who is suffering, someone who is pushing your limits, or simply someone who puts a neutral stop to maintaining correspondence or following through with a particular plan?

Is that suffering something you wanted to teach yourself? Would it affect the way you receive the words others are saying to you? And if you react imperfectly on your way towards accepting reality, isn't that just as acceptable since it's you anyway? The professor you expected would give you a break but instead went harder on you? That professor was You. Was he kind of right, though? Actually, yes. Humility lesson received. Thank you, thank you. Onto the next thing.

Expectations are an added weight we do not need to carry. We don't need to prove ourselves. Ever. Because doesn't it happen regardless? And doesn't it feel good to navigate the world in freedom of expectation from others? Isn't that one of the best gifts we can offer someone else who is doing their best to manage their life? Not poisoning them with our insecurities or burdening them with our needs *du jour*? There is always another path of least resistance. And if we're claiming this freedom for ourselves, and giving it to others—being one and the same—doesn't that sound like a dandy way to slowly and surely turn the world into a more peaceful, flowy, and enjoyable place?

Every little bit helps. Every lightness in interaction helps. Every *take your time, get back to me when you can, if it flows it flows, whatever you feel/want/need is okay* helps. Grab what sticks, allow the rest to crumble; it will make room to build the foundation and show you where it was weak.

Structures

> *It's not rocket science. It's social science — the science of understanding people's needs and their unique relationship with art, literature, history, music, work, philosophy, community, technology and psychology.*
> **CLEMENT MOK**

We need an awareness of structures in order to complete our frame of reference when we are analyzing relationships with others. People find refuge in the structures built around them, at times blindly accepting and reinforcing structures that no longer make sense because at one point these structures saved them, brought them comfort, got them through.

Structures can be the result of a traumatic event, created by those who needed them to survive the trauma. There can be cultural structures, such as when members of an entire society develop ways to cope during a war or political dictatorship and then remain influenced by the mindsets and behaviors that saved them. There can be family structures, where we are conditioned to accept certain traditions as certainties, governing our choices and shaping our adult identity around them.

> *Tolerance, openness and understanding towards other peoples' cultures, social structures, values and faiths are now essential to the very survival of an interdependent world.*
> **AGA KHAN IV**

People who grew up in Soviet countries had no food, no opportunities, and no freedom of expression for decades during communism.

During these harshest of times, they needed to rely on each other. I have many friends who lived through communism during their formative years and I have noticed there is a lasting effect on how friendship is defined. In Russia, a friend will give you her house, no questions asked, at any time you need. She will give you all her clothes, money, anything, because she understands what it means to have nothing and the need to survive. So a simple request to come visit you and stay for a while is completely normal, and it's more charged than the guest/host dynamics of Western Europeans. In a way, an Eastern European person is saying, "Come to my apartment for as long as you need so you won't die," versus "I'd be pleased if you stopped by on your way to Switzerland for dinner."

Once you realize this, you see the structure, you learn if it's not working for you, and you set your boundary. If it's not hurting you, you can accept it. Knowing this about post-communist survivors, can you really blame them for enjoying materialism? Is it a problem for you if your friend wants to dress up luxuriously and do elegant things? Completely rhetorical as it's really a personal choice.

One of my closest friends from college is Eastern European, and when we'd make plans for a simple dinner, she would come over and end up staying for days! And wear my clothes!! And tell me that I had run out of food (that of course we'd eaten). I loved her, but I would wonder why she didn't want to take some time for herself, wear her own clothes, and eat her own food. She could certainly afford it. But I was twenty and not yet well versed on boundaries, so I never said anything. To be honest, we had so much fun that I never cared — it was just unusual. It was the nature of our friendship. Years later, I went to visit her a couple of times. And during all of the times I visited her, she hosted me like I was her own sister. I never paid for a single meal, drink, or experience. It simply wasn't a question. This time I was on the opposite side and I felt slightly awkward. But now I get it. This is her way of communicating love. She grew up in a communist country where wealth and personal possessions were shared, where huddling together with five families in the only house on the street with working gas was the norm. I was fortunate to grow up in a free country, with my own playroom, and a keen awareness of mommy's private bath time and long-distance afternoon phone calls.

Structures can also be between husband and wife in the so-called gender roles in marriage, for example, when both believe and find refuge in maintaining traditional roles of breadwinner versus caregiver. This structure works if you are living in harmony. But let's look at two couples and in both cases the wife stays at home. One scenario is the result of a shared analysis and equitable division of responsibilities, where the couple leads a balanced and flexible lifestyle and it makes sense for the wife to stay home in their current situation — that's one approach of many and they both know this. A different scenario might be one where the husband "prefers" that his wife stay at home, and she married him because they both agreed to this blanket preference because it felt safe to them. What if suddenly this wife wanted to get a job? What if she wanted to invest in herself but silently agreed to put the family first? Wouldn't it make sense to expose the structure to her as her friend so that she could tear the structure down if she wanted to? Defending the structure over happiness is where the problem lies.

Relationships are complex and nuanced, just like the people in them. Recognizing structures will allow you to set the boundaries necessary for avoiding messy, enmeshed acquaintances that turn into friendships that end in a blowout.

We are all sailing in an ocean of social structures, navigating a careful dance between awareness and personal needs. When you are aware you are at the helm, you become responsible for leading the dance.

FRIENDSHIPS

*A friend is someone who knows
all about you and still loves you.*
ELBERT HUBBARD

We may not have grown up with the perfect family, but friends can become our family. Friendships are a vast category because they can range from the neighbor you just met in your new apartment building to the person you've known since you were two and tried alcohol with for the first time.

In the grand scheme of things, moments live forever. On a Soul level, the amount of time we've spent together in this lifetime is not necessarily a factor in the meaningfulness of a given friendship or acquaintance. (The cashier could have been your mother-in-law in a past life!) There are people we are meant to vibe with for a very long while in this lifetime because we aligned to know one another, and these friendships are gems to treasure. There are also people who come and go, making a great impact on our lives and then leave when it is time. *Poof.* The value of both experiences is equally immeasurable, they are impactful to us and our character just the same.

Nonetheless, the wonderful friendships I've experienced shared a few common traits. At times, we receive moments to capitalize on as lessons, even from our very own friends. If we have not yet solved some parts of us that are calling to be healed, a friend may come into our lives to teach us boundaries or ways to show up. And though perhaps, on the Soul level, we had agreed in advance for that challenge to happen, on the practical level we might not be ready to learn that lesson yet. So we move forward accordingly, without trying to change another's outcome, following the arrow of our truth.

Just like people and life circumstances, our friends are our mirrors. Through our interactions we are here to show them the best version of themselves and they to us. The mirror will also show us what we don't want to see. So we must be open to receiving that as well.

Lovely Friendships

> *Let us be grateful to people who make us happy, they are the charming gardeners who make our souls blossom.*
> **MARCEL PROUST**

A person who was once very close to me in life struggled very much with belonging and recognizing what incredible friends surrounded them. It was hard to get the message through. Words could not make up for their feeling of being judged and unworthy, and not a single friend of theirs could fill this void while they chose not to see it. It's not uncommon for us to be surrounded by blessings that we somehow cannot see. One could argue this observation applies to all of life. Focusing on what's lacking is certainly a recipe for living in lack.

On the other hand, those who have experienced the gentle love of a friend, the gracious support in times of need, and the growth that each person brings into our lives, are lucky folks indeed.

Real friendships do not judge, they are not envious, they are not controlling. Friendships do not play the zero sum game; they are abundant. There is no jealousy towards other friends, just a desire to help one another succeed.

There's truly a sense of non-judgment from a real friend. You can say anything and be anyone you are in that moment in full acceptance. If, of course, you learn first and foremost not to judge yourself.

Every snowflake is different, and so are we, and so are our friends. Each friend who walks beside us in life is an incredible manifestation of the love that we can also give and receive. If we choose to see friendship as an open flow of loving and receiving, then that is exactly what we will get. Whichever way we choose to see something, it becomes that choice.

> *A strong friendship doesn't need daily conversation or being together. As long as the relationship lives in the heart, true friends never part.*
> **ANONYMOUS**

It's also not realistic to be one-hundred-percent available and present in each of our friend's lives forever. Friendships go through phases. Understanding these waves and allowing them to come and go allows for an even greater ocean of love in your heart.

I see friends as angels that come to us on Earth to support us, challenge us to grow and give us a sense of belonging we may not otherwise have received from our immediate family structures. And this is what I hope I am to them.

> *Everyone has a friend during each stage of life. Some lucky ones have the same friend in all stages of life.*
> **ANONYMOUS**

Being a good friend means living in truth, being direct, being loving, and knowing how to receive that in return. Over time, our longest running friendships become anchors to help us remember who we truly are, and the new ones, a reflection of who we are becoming.

Boundaries

> *When we fail to set boundaries and hold people accountable, we feel used and mistreated. This is why we sometimes attack who they are, which is far more hurtful than addressing a behavior or a choice.*
> **BRENÉ BROWN**

Boundaries are important across all relationships, but their value kicks in even more when it comes to maintaining and growing good friendships.

Let's step back for a second. Let's go to a place where we are feeling fuzzy, and loving, and empowered, and everyone is elated in the friendship. This is the place to be! And this is the place to defend. Then something little happens that makes us uncomfortable, something very little. So little that we prefer to stretch the truth and stay in this place of idealized friendship a bit longer and choose not to see that something has happened to threaten this ideal.

We let it flow. We want things to sort themselves out. Love will conquer all, just be more compassionate, etc. etc. Not maliciously, but perhaps at our own expense, that person starts chipping off a bit more from our shoulder than we meant for them to take. Oops! They have no idea they are doing this, and you know they don't know, because they are your friend, they need you in some way and you know they are showing up in the best way they can. But at some point you notice you've stopped being real. You've accommodated a behavior at your own expense and now the shit is starting to accumulate in the fan.

I'm learning this in real time as I write this book, more than I ever have before: Boundaries are not to be feared, they are to be honored and brought to light for a purpose. Setting a boundary can be a vibe as well as a direct statement. Boundaries are building blocks to fulfilling your Purpose, your identity, your needs of the moment.

You must be discerning with your time and with your energy before your whole life passes and you've yet to become yourSelf.

You cannot be everything to everyone at all times. This is an easy statement to agree with, and most would. Until we step into real life and we think, *Okay, I'll just have a coffee with this person because it has been a long time.* Or, *Of course I'll help take a look at this document, they only need me for forty-five minutes.* Or, *Sure, I'll plan my evening around a video call, be there for the nth girls night out. What's the harm in validating their behavior once more? It's too much effort to say something now.* And somewhere along the way, you lose time, you lose the golden hours that were meant for you to create and shine, and you might start to resent your friend a little.

Everything should come from a place of good energy. No one can take away your energy unless you allow them to. Remember: It's really all your creation. It's common to feel that someone is trying to take advantage of you, and that the time has come to let them know! Oh yes, look at you now, rising and standing up for your rights. *GRR*! Tell them how important you are and how wrong it was for them to assume you'd be so available. *This will be great,* you think, *I will finally stake my claim. Then I will be stronger.* This is your ego wanting to be special, wanting to prove it was right to have gotten upset and how wrong others were to have put you in that position to begin with, to disrupt you from living important matters.

But that line of thinking is just inefficient and wrong! Inefficient because inevitably it hurts the friendship when you express yourself like this and wrong because it is being stated from a place of lack, and victimhood. You are blaming someone else for your limited resources, which are the same resources they have and neither of you has the power to make this otherwise. We all have the exact same hours in the day—this is a neutral and democratic fact. When you fail to create a boundary, you've simply allotted someone else's needs above your own. But how can you get upset with someone for doing exactly what you should be doing? Putting themselves first.

It's like you are all in one big spreadsheet, and you are placing column B (them) before column A (you). Perhaps column B is stated more clearly and urgently so your algorithm doesn't think to check column A for the answer first. That's a problem! Work on column A so you know what you need, and how much space you have left to welcome column B, and C, and D, E, F, G, etc.

Boundaries are there to help us defend the limited resources we have on this Earth. We came to this Earth to experience finiteness, duality, physical pleasure, social constructs, the taste of food, and a rich gamut of emotional states and nuances that our beautifully complete Souls do not have a need for in their light form.

You must take action to be in charge of your own wholeness. Your whole Self.

One of the best ways to learn about boundaries is to observe others who have them in place and watch how they operate. Boundaries are neutral statements, not attacking words. They go beyond pleasing or displeasing someone. In fact, the irony is we get blocked because we think we will displease someone, but the alternative brings the opposite—if we do not set boundaries, we are displeasing ourselves in favor of pleasing someone else.

None of that is good energy. The happy spot, the balance, is found in understanding and tweaking your own equation for input versus output, and gaining clarity on the action or behavior that is triggering you. It's helpful to make a quick pit stop within and calibrate before stating your boundary, because at first you may be feeling it in a heightened way emotionally. You can state the exact same words but if you are feeling down or defensive, they will vibrate differently than when you are once again in the driver's seat of your own car. When you're in the driver's seat, you can see the road ahead and can objectively anticipate whether a friend's request is appropriate based on the requirements of your exchange.

> *Boundaries we set for our life are important, life-saving even. A lot of hurt comes from allowing others to guilt us into breaking them.*
> **ZARA HAIRSTON**

There may, of course, be times where the need to set a boundary catches you off guard or on a day where everything seems to be falling apart. In those cases, the fact you've stated the boundary supersedes the style of its less-than-stellar delivery. You may have been driven to this point and not known how to express yourself. The trust and friendship built over time become a padded landing for these small crashes. Nobody is perfect and it is ultimately our thoughtful, non-judging friends with whom we should feel comfortable being real, and occasionally losing it.

Here's an example. Someone has been asking for your advice a lot, and you've been giving it because you're happy to; that's what friends do. Actually, it's rather flattering to think someone listens to your advice this much. But now it's getting to be a lot more than you thought it would be, the messages are getting longer and longer, and this person seems to need you for most decisions. You go about trying to live your day, and when you see the messages come in, you reluctantly open them because how can you not? The friend begins calling you—every morning, every night. Just for about ten or fifteen minutes. They really need you!

But they do not. **You are not so important to fixing them**; they need themSelves. **You are too important to fix them**; you need yourSelf. And the result of both of you recognizing how much you can do for yourselves apart from each other is the start of a new healing process. Yes, it risks short-term disappointment, but as the boundary-setter, you can bring healing into your friendship. To set a boundary in favor of cultivating a better relationship is an honorable intention indeed. Boundaries are an opening to create more room for understanding, collaboration, and personal growth.

Simple boundary rules:

- Thank the person for reaching out to you, for thinking of you.

- Thank them for what it is they are asking you, and let them know if you can or cannot help.

- If you cannot help, let them know why (timing, appropriateness, your plate is full, energy exchange is not in balance).

- Give them the chance to accept or challenge your boundary with their own. *Is this okay for you to speak about later? Am I missing an important piece of information?*

- If they challenge you on your boundary, you reevaluate with the new information.

- Always address the facts and do not vilify the person. It's not you versus them. Remove the ego from your interaction.

And remember, if someone gets upset with you because you set a boundary, then that boundary was probably needed. Do not be afraid to adjust from time to time, like you would a painting hanging on the wall; keep yourself centered.

Ending Friendships

> *One always has to know when a stage comes to an end. If we insist on staying longer than the necessary time, we lose the happiness and the meaning of the other stages we have to go through.*
> **PAULO COELHO**

In closing cycles, you may feel like you are closing down options and opportunities. In reality, you are making room for something even better—more things to come your way that are in alignment with you.

Sometimes boundaries are not enough, or we may have failed in setting them appropriately over time. After a series of jumbled misunderstandings and mutated silences, we find that we are no longer able to maintain a friendship with someone. They could also be feeling this way about us. *Who knows.*

Maybe, maybe, maybe.

We live in a world where pain and suffering are still normalized, unexposed, and perpetuated. There can come a point in a friendship where it is necessary to take a break, to remove oneself from the cycles of unhealthy patterns that have accumulated from your combined energies. It might be time to pull the break or make an exit if someone's pain is manifesting in a way that you cannot justify its deliberate affliction on you, or the person doesn't seem remorseful for inflicting such aggression and misery, or they aren't willing to work together towards a solution. Ask yourself if this is you towards another person. It can also be you!

It's easy to blame and become offended in the heat of things, but this isn't high school. Beautiful adult friendships of mine have ended without someone being bad and someone being good. They ended respectfully, without the desire to destroy one another or each other's reputations among our common friends. Our friendship came to be this way when neither one of us was willing to compromise on newly discovered, unshared principles of truth.

And the reason for this is not because many different truths exist. What is truth but confirmation of itself? Truth is an indisputable, direct message of the heart connected to the Universe we All share. No, the friendship ended due to one or both of us being unconsciously trapped in one or more untruths we genuinely believed to be true at the time.

When we recognize someone is hiding behind a structure, or missing parts of the story, putting themselves and you in the middle of their suffering, we can try to help them. But unless they choose to see it themselves and recognize there is something holding them back, they are saying, "Take me and take my skewed version of reality or leave." The minute you identify a structure is the moment you know you are not in it, and you owe it to yourself not to feed into the other person's torment if that is the cost of keeping the relationship alive.

Never sacrifice your own beliefs in the name of a friendship that is half blind to the truth. It's a lot of effort to validate someone's unnecessarily painful vision of the world; especially if that means you need to tiptoe around their vision, mildly ascribe to it, and even apologize for things you have done with only the best intentions.

It comes down to needs and to understanding which of them are fair and which needs are putting you or someone else in a sticky situation that could easily heal by acknowledging why those situations happen.

WORK

> *Company cultures are like country cultures. Never try to change one. Try, instead, to work with what you've got.*
> **PETER F DRUCKER**

As you might remember from the beginning of this journey, work is something I've done a lot of, particularly in what we'd refer to as the corporate world.

We will be discussing work in the business context, since this is where I have the most to contribute and where relationship "rules" thrive the most. Work itself, as a general concept, is a beautiful part of life, it helps us feel fulfilled and purposeful and allows us to eat, live, reproduce, travel, etc.

Work *relationships* are funny because they can feel super real, and during the moment you are in them they take up a great majority of your time — more so than a friendship would at some points in adulthood. Yet, just like a proper dinner setting requires you to mind your p's and q's and understand how to place your cutlery when you have finished eating, work relationships also have their etiquette.

This is not an all-inclusive explanation of work relationships. If you own your own company, or you're creating a super cool startup, or maybe you're a ski instructor, freelancer, or actor, or you earn your livelihood by exploring marine biology across the world, then this part may or may not be for you. I am referring to the work context I know — the corporate-ish one, where things have started or are already quite expanded, and people automatically fall into certain roles within somewhat pre-established cultural expectations (in the Western Hemisphere).

Still, there will be parts that apply to all working relationships, and the possible complications that could arise when you ruffle your featherbottom against the featherbottom of a fellow collaborator.

Dealing With a Difficult Boss

> *Quitting because you don't want to be uncomfortable will prevent you from growing.*
> **AMY MORIN**

Being too quick to end a work relationship that we chose for ourselves puts us in danger of encountering the same situation in a variety of ways later, and makes us escape from what that relationship could be teaching us.

It is often said that people do not leave because of their jobs, they leave because of the people. What makes it tricky is that, by definition, superiors have more influence than us, and the relationships we develop with our bosses are arguably the most impactful relationships we have at work. If we find ourselves in a challenging dynamic, sustaining this relationship can take a lot of energy. However, once we understand what is happening, there's always a way to grow better and stronger from it.

Before we get started, a quick self-reflection is in order. We must ask ourselves: Are we playing by the rules? Are we meeting deadlines, putting forth our best effort, and generally feeling good in our conscience regarding the objective value of our contributions? Self-reflection is an important step to assess with honesty. Feeling a bit demotivated at work is understandable, but passive-aggressive behaviors that impact our performance are not part of the solution.

It's normal for a challenging dynamic to be emotionally difficult to control. When people trigger each other, there are corresponding parts inside each of them asking to be seen and healed. Sometimes these triggers open past wounds we've merely put band-aids over since childhood for our own survival. And because they've been buried so deeply, they have now mutated into this form in order to rise to the surface.

There is likely an underlying karmic reason, as well. The Souls could have made an agreement where one said, "I'll make you uncomfortable in such and such ways so that you may grow," and the other Soul responds, "I'll do it back to you so that you may grow in such and such ways." And so it happens, and there it is. A growth lesson.

But the question remains: what is this situation here to teach us? That is the starting point.

While acknowledging there is an active lesson and opportunity for healing, our biggest priority should be maintaining and defending our inner peace. Being gentle with ourselves is a necessary part of coping. This may require extra self-care in our personal lives, planning fun experiences with friends, benevolent distractions, and moments of novelty to keep our spirits up. The way to transmute a low vibration is to think or do its opposite. If the opposite of our low vibration doesn't happen automatically, then we need to actively pursue it.

What might a difficult relationship with a boss or superior look like? Well, anything we feel is impacting our ability to operate freely on a task, when the weight of a negative emotion behind the task is greater than what the task calls for. A difficult relationship with a superior can show up as mistrust, micromanaging, shaming in front of other team members, a refusal to acknowledge fair victories, disrespecting boundaries, withholding information, or envy after idealizing to an uncomfortable extreme. In the worst cases, a difficult relationship can even lead to sabotage. These are some examples of the outer experience.

When things escalate—and they will do just that if they go unaddressed—it could start to feel like we are under attack at work. Low-key episodes of acute attacks.

We may feel confused, because we *want* to be wrong about it. It's tempting to engage in denial, wishing we could go about our day just like every other Tom and Joe. But guess what? It affects us. In fact, one of the symptoms of a problematic dynamic in the workplace is that it starts to bleed into our personal lives. We catch ourselves thinking about the situation outside of work. It becomes an unhealthy obsession—the perceived unfairness of it all is consuming to the reacting mind.

We must remove ourselves from that unproductive space. We are here to learn! We can ask ourselves these questions instead: What is this situation making me feel? When did I first feel this way? What about this dynamic resembles that time and what makes it different this time? Can I go back in time to the moment this first happened and hug that little child and let them know everything is okay? Can I separate myself from feeling unnecessary pain simply by recognizing that this is a pattern playing out for me in order to help me heal?

All the medicine we need can only come from us, and this is another test to prove it. Remember: You are the solution!

What if we are in the middle of being attacked and on the verge of quitting immediately?

If we are driving through a storm, hail, snow, wind, muddy puddles, all these things can affect our driving, so it's good to be cautious in how we steer the vehicle and aware of what could damage us. But we keep going; the destination remains in sight. Our job is the vehicle. Our Soul is the driver.

After we overcome the storm, that's when we regroup, check the map, and evaluate a new destination. Never jump out of a moving vehicle.

Then, and only then, should we evaluate if it's the right time to leave.

When both people have regained composure, and driven out a bit further than the eye of the storm, *that* is the time to discern what is best. And the other party, in this case your boss, is free to choose whether or not they will take the lesson. You can say this to anyone with whom you've ridden a storm with: *I honor the path you take, even if you choose the path of least resistance. Thank you, thank you, thank you for the opportunity to learn from you. I choose peace now, and new growth.*

And guess what? You may even become great friends later and laugh about the times you've challenged one another.

Which is why you always leave on a good note. Always leave with your own smile. Always leave with closure and lessons learned. Never before. The Universe has an unlimited amount of people and scenarios to bring us back to the lesson in case we leave earlier.

Being a Good Boss

> *The best executive is the one who has sense enough to pick good men to do what he wants done, and self-restraint to keep from meddling with them while they do it.*
> **THEODORE ROOSEVELT**

Being a good boss is easy. Here's how:

- Be good at your job.
- Be kind to your subordinates.
- Trust.
- Respect.
- Let them shine and align.

When people come to work for you, be aware that they are there on borrowed time. Your first job is to identify whether you are on a path to support each other. You're giving them employment and they're giving you their time and dedication, but in addition to this there is a far greater energy exchange. For things to run smoothly, you must trust them to do their magic in whichever form it comes. Otherwise, why would you have hired someone else and not just done the job yourself?

> *Feel yourself being an opening through which energy flows from the unmanifested Source of all life through you for the benefit of all.*
> **ECKHART TOLLE**

Of course, it is your company, and of course results matter, but you need to be open to what someone else can teach you so that you can grow and improve, which is the ultimate goal.

Some people teach you to grow, and in that case, you are there to give them guidance and fill their cups with knowledge and experience. Others are perfectly content to support you and not grow. Some will come to you to help you move, disrupt, enhance, and if you trust them, you need to let them spread their wings or let them go like free birds. These are the people that will help you avoid stagnation.

Once you've formed your employees on the vision of your company, *they* become contributors to the vision-keeping with the added value of their own perspective. You, in turn, provide them with the encouragement to be themselves. If they've proven their candidacy, the best thing you can do is watch what they can do and get as much out of their way as possible.

> *A good boss makes his men realize they have more ability than they think they have so that they consistently do better work than they thought they could.*
> **CHARLES ERWIN WILSON**

You celebrate and reinforce the positive. There is no reason to talk down to someone after an error, as errors are appropriately internalized by a virtuous person with a pure heart. You just reason through it. The punishment will have already occurred within their own internal processing. What you must do is praise each other when you do well, energize each other by saying how you see that person bettering things, and encourage each other to bring more light and more unique energy into their creations.

We are all creators, and if we cannot create something of our own, we need to be free to create for others. Outside of their assigned goals, give employees space to do something of their own. Set aside a few hours per week for each employee to do something they feel would be right for the company, whatever that may be, and if their project fails, okay, no problem, next. This will foster confidence, autonomy, and drive in your company. All of which are key and necessary ingredients to create a sustainable, motivating vibe. And if your company succeeds and produces revenue, allow them to be a part of that! I'd go as far as to say split it. But don't tell them at first, make it a surprise. A delightful surprise.

This is how you shape talent: You hold the space to generate and manifest so that people around you can thrive. Together you go up. But separate you go…separately.

I have found—both as an employee and a boss—that this attitude improves moods and increases productivity in a healthy, exciting way. If you choose to lead with fear instead, blaming and belittling human errors, being suspicious of people's intentions, and expecting the worst to happen when they are left unsupervised, you will get exactly that.

Coworkers

> *If you want to work in corporate, then you should know how to play chess.*
> **ANONYMOUS**

I am quite confident that someone starting their own company or working with friends will be able to take a voyeuristic view of this section. I also hope that soon we will be moving towards a world where etiquette and social strategies such as these will not need to be implemented. However, if you do join a corporate structure, you have to play the game. And *this*, my dear friends, is a bit of how the game is played. If you're not playing it, someone else will be, so you may as well choose the style of your player.

Navigating coworkers is similar to finding your niche in high school or college. You want to find the right table to eat lunch at, sure, but you're now evaluating people's coolness differently. At work you can't just ignore people, you have to work at every relationship and assess the degree to which it will promptly move your player through the game.

Rule number 1: Always say less than you feel and do not overshare. Not *shy*, but private.

Remember that everyone, or most, here are motivated by financial reward.

In a simplified, mind-oriented manner of speaking (and traditional workspaces *are* governed by mind-oriented relationships), your coworkers can be segmented as overall *positive, neutral, negative or "work friends."* You want to surround yourself with neutral and positive people and keep the negatives to a bare minimum. Let's go through each of these so you can spot them in your workplace.

The *Positives* are helpful, upbeat, and enjoyable. They may not work *with* you but they are in your periphery. You'll want to keep them around to happily distract yourself. These are the people you send an air high-five to on your way to the coffee room and sometimes share interdepartmental meetings with. Perhaps they were in your orientation group when you first joined the company. You sometimes get lunch with Positives, and because of their nature, it's usually with a bunch of other people as well.

Neutrals are efficient people who are always pleasant to talk to, but you sort of feel like if you had stayed one more second at their desk, you would have annoyed them. They are polite, helpful, and solid members of the company. They just aren't comfortable being your friend.

The *Negatives* are the downers. They don't know how to read social cues, so conversations with them can be downright painful. Or they are simply negative people—energy vampires always wanting to talk about what's not working in the company, their dissatisfaction with management, etc. This can be hard when they are direct coworkers you cannot avoid who, because they happen to be very talented in what they do, are "tolerated" at the expense of good, positive people. Which is unfortunate. But this is the game, and this is what you signed up for. You won't be alone in these revelations, and you can find comfort in that. If you need them to accomplish your own tasks, then email them and keep conversation task-oriented. If you see them trying to talk to you about negative things, abort the mission and call in the boundaries.

Work Friends are like positive colleagues, but as the term implies, they are more. Work Friends are those you can tell everything to and you feel safe with them. You can overdrink together at happy hour and share who has slept with whom, who you like personally, and other deeper and darker secrets that only they can appreciate by working in your same environment.

If you're lucky, the people you interact with on a daily basis are either neutral, positive, or work friends. If you meet someone negative, who tends to speak badly about the office, avoid them. Or get really good at cutting them off, because whether they're right or wrong, you don't have time for that kind of energy. Nor do you want to be seen with them if they have this reputation.

You want to be non-ironically and matter-of-factly enthused to grow with the company forever, naturally attracting and interacting with those who have this outlook as well, while at the same time not being too extra about it.

This attitude will also get you far when negotiating for higher salaries and roles. You want to repeat statements like, "I feel that in five years my value will grow in this direction," or "I am really attracted to the project because it will sharpen these skills that I intend to give back in such and such ways as I continue to demonstrate my worth."

Snug as a bug in a corporate rug.

Do as much as you can to also learn as many administrative and organizational capabilities as possible, since these skills will always be useful.

PART 3

RELATIONSHIP WITH THE UNIVERSE

CHAPTER 5

UNIVERSAL LAWS

Do not make the mistake of supposing that the little world you see around you — the Earth, which is a mere grain of dust in the Universe — is the Universe itself. There are millions upon millions of such worlds, and greater. And there are millions of millions of such Universes in existence.

THE KYBALION

For real, it's like that. It *could* be like that. And understanding the vastness of this concept can be both comforting and unsettling, depending on the day.

The Kybalion is a compilation of Hermetic teachings written in the early 1900s by three anonymous individuals known as the Three Initiates. Everything I've written in this book falls in alignment with the seven Hermetic principles found in The Kybalion. I recommend that anyone curious to explore basic principles of Universal Law and esoteric philosophy read The Kybalion or listen to the audio recording. Briefly, the seven principles are listed here.

1. THE PRINCIPLE OF MENTALISM

"The All is Mind, the Universe is Mental."

Alas, we've found a noble purpose for the mind! Without our mind's consciousness, we wouldn't be able to conceive the existence of the Universe and the concept of the All. The formless form, the causeless cause, the existence before Creation. The All is all-encompassing of both what *is* and what *is not*, because within All exists the non-existent. All is All. In order to comprehend this, we need the mind.

The principle of mentalism helps us answer questions like:

- What can I learn from the experience?
- Why am I projecting this experience?
- What am I seeing through this prism?

2. THE PRINCIPLE OF CORRESPONDENCE

"As above, so below."

As within, so without; as the Universe, so the Soul. Our Souls are both a part of and a container for the Universe, and the Universe contains our Soul. The world around us is a manifestation of our world within. What we give in this world isn't what we are going to get, it is what we expect, and what happens to us happens to others. Everything is affected.

As Rumi said, "*You are the mighty ocean in a drop.*"

Imagine the power of all the oceans coming together.

3. THE PRINCIPLE OF VIBRATION

"Nothing rests; everything moves; everything vibrates."

Everything in the Universe, whether it is physical or mental, has a vibration. The second you have a thought, it's given a vibration. The more it's thought about, the more charge it's given to become real.

"The atom of matter, the unit of force, the mind of man and the being of the archangel are but one degree in one scale, and all fundamentally the same. The difference being between solely a matter of degree, and rate of vibration."

Everything in the Universe is the same thing but vibrating at different speeds. You can change yourself through your vibration. Raising vibration can happen by closing our eyes in meditation. This gives a whole new experience of life. No matter what happens to you, you can raise your vibration. If you want to see love, be Love. Your vibration then impacts the experience of the world around you, and you'll stop feeding into previous loop cycles.

4. THE PRINCIPLE OF POLARITY

"Everything is dual; everything has poles; everything has its pair of opposites; like and unlike are the same; opposites are identical in nature, but different in degree; extremes meet; all truths are but half-truths; all paradoxes may be reconciled."

All opposites are different ends of the same pole. Heat and cold are both temperatures.

"Where does 'darkness' leave off, and 'light' begin?"

Does the Earth spin counterclockwise or clockwise? It depends. South Pole and North Pole determine a different answer. The reference point changes your perception, and even perception is polarized.

If you want to change your state, concentrate on the opposite pole of polarity. Kill the undesirable by changing its polarity.

5. THE PRINCIPLE OF RHYTHM

> *"Everything flows, out and in; everything has its tides; all things rise and fall; the pendulum-swing manifests in everything; the measure of the swing to the right is the measure of the swing to the left; rhythm compensates."*

Everything has its ebb and flow. For every action there is an equal and opposite reaction.

We can't stop the principle of rhythm because we cannot compete with the Higher Order. But we can raise our vibrations by focusing on a more desirable state to embody.

6. THE PRINCIPLE OF CAUSE AND EFFECT

> *"Every cause has its effect; every effect has its cause; everything happens according to law; chance is but a name for law not recognized; there are many planes of causation, but nothing escapes the law."*

Nothing happens without reason, there's a principle of cause and causation and everything that happens is following the law of cause and effect. You might not directly know the cause of an effect happening to you. The cause may have happened on a different plane of existence, on a macro pattern, but there's no such thing as chance or coincidence.

The future determines the past and the past determines the future.

7. THE PRINCIPLE OF GENDER

"Gender is in everything; everything has its masculine and feminine principles; gender manifests on all planes."

There are masculine and feminine qualities behind all things and people, which are in each of them to create balance in the world. Both are necessary and symbiotic. The emotional fluidity of the Moon is needed to guide the manifesting strength of the Sun. Without each other they are incomplete, and similarly this applies to you and your complete beingness. Look beyond biology.

Connected to the Universe, we are an infinitely unique multiplicity of gender. Ishtar and Athena are goddesses of sexual love and war. We need logic and intuition, brain and heart, action and rest, and so on and so forth.

• • •

When we begin to awaken to the Universal forces that work for and with us and learn to decode the language that speaks to us every day, we activate and open our senses to live in a state of Truth and flow.

This awareness comes with a variety of side effects: our sensitivity is enhanced, what is seen cannot be unseen, what is learned cannot be unlearned, and often we will be pushing our own boundaries if we wish to follow the laws of the greater order. Doing this creates true growth. However, we have free choice. We can always push pause on our growth and watch Netflix all day, or not speak up, or not cancel our plans at the last minute if they don't resonate.

Yet! If we do choose to go with the guidance of the Universe, and if we do choose to make a statement or speak up for what we want, then a funny thing happens: We tend to get what we want! If we properly understand the laws that exist for our highest good, we will get exactly what we need.

CHAPTER 6

ENERGY

When the energy is directed outside, you create and manifest life outside, and when the same energy is directed inward, you reach to the ultimate truth of life.

ROSHAN SHARMA

Waking up to this Higher Order can be scary at first. For anyone currently undergoing the process of awakening, I want to share an excerpt of what I wrote to a teacher during my initial awakening process. Following this, we will go directly into discussing our relationships with three components that energetically guide our destiny on this Earth: Money, Manifesting, and Being Real.

About a year ago when I began an active exploration into the Universe, I started to feel very awake for hours in the night. It was powerful and awe inspiring, I would look at the sky wide awake and feel this immensity overcoming me. We really are active players in this beautiful plan of self-transformation. Life is so beautifully more, and how strange few can see this. I would notice disappointed faces of city people around me and just wish they could see. Life is not this serious! How can you not see? This compassion overcame me. Oh humanity, look within, when will you wake up? I would pray for them to have strength.

Then this energy continued to keep me up and it spooked me. A lot. At the same time I felt emptiness. This Aloneness, this realization that if the Universe is within us, and we are part of it, at some point we continue to transform, and perhaps at the end of it all, does all get swallowed by nothingness? Is nothingness the end goal? And then is all we have our own awareness? Then I didn't feel held, I felt disenchanted and very scared. The energy was so strong. Surrounding me. I was as awake as I would be at noon on a sunny day for nights in a row.

I had to ask them to please let me feel like a human being who knows nothing again. Leave me alone! And for a little bit I could sleep. I found an equilibrium. They help me now to understand what it is I need in the Universe, through me, and whether there is purpose in what I am doing. Whatever this purpose is, it is Truth, and I am called to put this above all else. Sometimes I succeed, other times I do not, but I always know which is which.

MONEY

> *We have to survive. You have to manage your relationships, you have to manage your things, and if you do it the right way, everything falls in place.*
> **MY GRANDMOTHER JACQUELINE**

I love my grandmother. She is practical and wise. And beyond the material needs for survival that we have, many of our blocks in this physical world come from the way we approach, hold, and spend money. We all have that one friend (or perhaps it's you?) who counts money a little too much, or takes note of the decimal at the end of a bill.

Notice how perhaps that person isn't living in prosperity or abundance? They may have a nice big house and many wonderful experiences in their lives, but deep down, is that person really free when they are counting pennies and overthinking every single financial transaction they make?

Money is energy and we have it to make things happen around us, to help us manifest our dreams, to amplify our reach. Therefore, money is very closely connected with the Universal exchange.

> *Wealth is your perception of possibility and opportunity that is available to you. People set that limit themselves.*
> **ENVITA ROSE HASLER**

When someone has an expanded mindset, they can help others. And that is when the real ripple effect picks up its momentum and goes into action!

Energy Exchange

> *Money, like all life, is an energy exchange. You give yourself over to whatever you're passionate about, and what comes back to you is energy in the form of monetary compensation. You attract more or less of what you want by how you choose to interact with it, as well as what you believe about yourself. Do you truly feel you deserve what you're asking for? Are you worth it? How you answer impacts what comes your way.*
>
> **ALICIA KEYS**

Money is the intermediary to an action, it's an attention grabber, it's freedom from the shackles of someone else's control. Money can be so many things, but most of all it is an energy exchange.

The numerical value we give to money is secondary when our Soul wants something. Before money, water was an energy exchange. Harvest was an energy exchange, and so was cattle. These resources provided survival and determined the success of a community.

When I was a child, my father bought me a small Louis Vuitton purse during one of his business trips. I remember he told me this was a very special purse, a very fashionable sign of elegance, and to treat it well. I'm going to be honest, I thought he was kidding. A brown purse? Brown on brown? That purse had value for me because it was a gift from my father, not because it was a Louis Vuitton, but I used it when I pretended to be an old lady during playtime. Sometimes I liked to play that I was an orphan girl from Oliver Twist, this was my purse for that. Do you know what had value to me? The pink, glittery, transparent plastic purse that came with my princess sticker collection.

Value is about what speaks to your heart.

Have you ever had moments in which you wanted to do something from your heart and you decided to take a leap and make the expense, then somehow that amount came back to you?

That's how money works. It's energy. It finds its way to you when you are aligned with your true purpose, and you need not worry about the outcome if your purchase is an expense that will give you the opportunity to expand yourself. The amount of money is just a coincidence, a societal translation of arbitrary value. Your unique path will gravitate towards what needs to be leveraged in you. You just need to choose if you are ready and if it's right for you.

> *What we really want to do is what we are really meant to do. When we do what we are meant to do, money comes to us, doors open for us, we feel useful, and the work we do feels like play to us.*
> **JULIA CAMERON**

One time I spent €9,000 on personal development and energy healing. This was a BIG expense for me! Holy moly, I couldn't believe it. I hesitated, questioned, worried. But what allowed me to go forward was the following thought: *What could be safer than investing in myself?* Scary question! And the ultimate apprehension behind every thought was: *If this fails, if I fail at achieving my dream after taking this leap, that would make me the only one to blame.* But then again, aren't we always the only ones to blame for what we create despite the veils and layers of context we drape around ourselves?

We can expand through knowledge (pursuing studies or going to a conference), through experience (going on a trip or signing up for a spiritual retreat), or through an investment in yourself (asking for a loan to invest in a home or your business).

Three weeks after I chose to work with this incredible healer, I received €11,000 in my bank account. It was truly unexpected and it blew me away. I don't mean to sound like I am selling smoke here, nor am I stating that unicorns and fairies are real (although, yes!) — the money came from my former job. It was just unexpected.

When you are in alignment and all you need is money to fulfill your goal, you mustn't be too concerned about it, nor intimidated by the quantity. (What if you were meant to do something great? You! Yeah, you!) If we vibrate in the frequency of what we *can* do, not from the place of what we are missing, this shifts the energy. Of course, this energy shift requires that we work on ourselves to be in tune with our hearts. So, if you are even just a little bit there, and have just enough trust, if the only thing stopping you from pursuing that next thing is your own ability to follow up on an expense and follow through with being great (don't be afraid of being great), then go for it! And do it with open arms. Perhaps it will work out the first time, or it will not, but keep going and the results will come.

Try this approach with little things. Invest in something you need that you would have otherwise sacrificed because it seemed like it would be a "waste" of money, something that makes your Soul happy. The more you witness how it works, the more you will be in the flow.

Amplifier

Money and success don't change people; they merely amplify what is already there.
WILL SMITH

Money can amplify our creative power and our choices in life. Money helps us carry out our missions. It is a very precious tool that enhances our self-realization on this Earth.

Energetically, just like the Universe, money is neutral. We are the ones to project significance onto it. It can turn happy and aligned people into great people, and it can turn sad and misguided people into worse people. Money allows us to access opportunities we wouldn't have had without it. A whole world can open up!

So, money amplifies who we are and impacts what we do. If we are well intentioned with our money, we will inherently give and spread more good with it. If we are bitter, miserable, blocked people who do not act from the heart and are not motivated by pureness, these negative sides will be amplified onto the rest of the world in our dealings with money.

When we accept money from questionable sources, we must additionally pay attention to the charge with which it comes to us. For example, say you know someone who has been battling a difficult divorce settlement and they are down to the final dollars. This person decides to fight to the bitter end to get an additional few hundred dollars. If we decide to exchange money with this angry and resentful person, what kind of charge will come with it? Something to pay attention to in your interactions, and then make a free choice about.

Not everyone is meant to have millions of dollars, simply because some people wouldn't even be comfortable with that amount. If you aren't willing to compromise yourself, the Universe will give you exactly what you need because the money that flows with the Universe to you is money that comes from a good energetic place.

But nobody is saying this path is easy!

Humor me: It's easy to be a jerk and have lots of money and neglect your inner wisdom, and it's easy to be a spiritual person with a good heart and have no money. Try being highly spiritual, with an open heart, with money. It's a great responsibility and takes work! It takes a lot of integration, constant self-discovery, and discernment. But it's worth it, if you need it for your mission.

It's not easy to leave the cocoon of the forest to go into the city, or trade the comfort of internal reflection for the hustle and bustle of external stimuli, but this is how we keep the balance of the pendulum swing. The eternal perfection and wholeness we witness in the ethereal realm is intoxicating, and it is the truth, but it is not our earthly reality, nor is it why we came here. Bridging this gap is where we all will meet for the next phase of growth in human consciousness.

Relationship With Money

Money is attracted, not pursued.
JIM ROHN

Just like people in questionable relationships, money doesn't necessarily go where it is needed and desperately desired. It goes where it is attracted. Rejecting it or coveting it will give you extreme outcomes that are not in the flow of abundance.

Just because you *need* a boyfriend or girlfriend, does that mean you will get one? Or the right one, for that matter? Needing and wanting something come from a place of lack. A person coming from a place of romantic scarcity might say things like, "Poor me, I am alone, I need someone beside me. Why is it that everyone has a partner and I don't?" Would you be attracted to such a person?

Now replace those statements of romantic scarcity with statements from money scarcity. "Poor me (literally), I don't have any money, I need money in my life. Why is it that everyone seems to have enough money and I don't?"

Money is not attracted to this vibe. Notice how even a very good poor person isn't able to make ends meet, despite living an honest life and praying every day for money to come to their family. They certainly deserve it! They're like the nice guy who never gets a girlfriend, eventually making statements like, "The world is unfair, I don't get what I am doing wrong."

Blaming the external is not how it works. The energy of money goes where it is desired, just like in a relationship. It goes to those who respect it, who embrace it to bring forth what they believe to be even stronger than themselves. Money is not a possession, it's an ally with whom to carry out courageous plans.

Money doesn't go to fear, unworthiness, or neediness, because if we were to strip everything away we truly do not need anything and we are worthy of it all. When you start counting pennies, it's just like being controlled in a relationship. Money dislikes that energy as much as you do! Money is lighter, it's freer, it flows.

It's there to be passed around and poured into the glasses of those with whom you are sharing your meal of life.

And sure, you can use it to invest in a home, put together a contract, and ensure that the agreements are tidy — that is fine and dandy, but be cool about it. Leave it flexible. Always have a way out. Mortgage agreements end when you sell the house, or after thirty years. Marriages can be concluded. Maintain your identity, and know that if you keep walking your path in truth and gratitude, with as little worry as possible, in trust, making choices in alignment with your energy and understanding the power and responsibility of amplification, the Universe will provide you with exactly what you need, perhaps something even better and different than what you initially thought you wanted.

Abundance is not something we acquire.
It is something we tap into.
WAYNE DYER

MANIFESTING

Whatever you can do, or dream you can, begin it. Boldness has genius, power, and magic in it. Begin it now.
JOHANN WOLFGANG VON GOETHE

All things must first exist in thought before they become a reality; this is the law of attraction. All is open. All you have to do is dream it to be true. When you dream it, it lives inside of you.

We come from a place where everything we could possibly want is already a part of us and we lack nothing. In this place of abundance, manifestation is as normal as sneezing in April. Before we came to this world as our physical Selves, we were non-physical energetic Beings connected to Source. We had no notion of separation because we were the Whole. In this state, we knew that entering a physical body would require choices, and we chose to experience this reality.

Dreams really do come true when they come from a place that is pure and light—as long as we know what we want and are willing to put in the right amount of work to achieve our dreams. Through manifesting, we become confident without pressure. Playfully sure. The Earth becomes our playground! Our Souls are here to play, learn, and expand.

You can practice manifesting little things by being in a good vibe. You'll start to notice that things start flowing for you. Maybe you get a free donut, or the waitress intuitively knows you wanted lemon, or maybe you find a parking spot right up front, or maybe your train miraculously makes it on time (unless you live in Switzerland, in which case this is not a miracle). Concentrate on something you'd like, then be grateful as if you already have it. Then be okay without it, knowing that if you had it, it would be wonderful, so why not request it? You'd be free to do more.

Say you are an actor going to your second audition. Clearly they liked you. You are one of two or three up for the role, and you really are perfect for it. You can feel it. It could change your life, and launch you into huge stardom. Good. Are you ready? Do not fear your fears, doubt your doubts! Challenge the challenge with the strength of your inner light. It's not about ego, it's about alignment. You must especially want and be ready for the good, too! Believe you are worthy to receive, and it will be so. Either this time or one soon after.

There are many things we think we want in life, but do we really want all of it? Do we want all that comes with our desired goal? The unwavering commitment and no turning back that comes with making that choice? We must constantly check within for blocks preventing us from manifesting the desired result. Along the way of achieving something great are many little windows of action and meetings and dialogues that are there to inform us whether or not we are on track.

Until the Universe recognizes that we are totally clear and committed on what we envision for ourselves, it will not give us that which we ask for because it cannot interpret a confusing request. What will you do with extra money if you aren't prepared for a change? Buy a boat? Be rich? Okay, but you will still embody the same unawareness as before, just with that new possession. And, of course, with a lot less energy because you will never catch up when going against your flow.

> *When any one of us is aligned with our purpose, there is an inexhaustible source of energy. Once you're aligned with your purpose, the energy is always there to do whatever you need. You never get tired, and you do everything with a sense of joy. It's actually effortless – it's a flow.*
> **DENNIS KUCINICH**

We can achieve what we want through shortcuts, manipulations, or even a head-down, sheer willingness to work hard, but those approaches are not the same as achieving what we want through alignment. Until we are fully committed and ready to put our names on all that comes with the process, big blessings cannot be released. We will get affirmations and reminders that we are on the right path, and little chances to jump here and there, but the full manifestation of our dreams comes from the full realization of our worth to receive it and start going. Across all dimensions.

Success can be just as partial as your intentions. Partiality can manifest but you miss out on something when it is not achieved with the fullness of your whole Self. You miss out on fully enjoying the blessing when it comes to you and the wholeness you feel when you can appreciate it, and the freedom of not attaching to it.

What is it about that project that isn't getting you to be fully invested in it? Is it you? Is it your intention with it? Are you already rushing towards the finish line without appreciating the middle? What is your level of commitment? Are you willing to go to jail for that cause? Are you trying to skip the middle and avoid the internal journey you're on? Are you trying to shorten the journey you need to prepare for your greatness? If you skip a lesson, you will be met with it again later, and greater.

There are no shortcuts. There are no coincidences. There are no wrong turns. In the end, all paths converge.

Trust in the wisdom of the Greater Order, the unknown. Trust in your ability to manifest what is beautiful and meant for you. And do pay attention along the way.

Faith

> *Ask once, believe you have received, and all you have to do to receive is feel good.*
> **RHONA BYRNE**

There are times to ask the questions, and times to know when to stop asking questions. Times when the answers have already been shown to you in a plethora of ways because you've done the work. When you are doing the work, all that is left to do is to have Faith.

This is a beautiful place to be.

Asking *too many* questions to the Universe is like finding the right perfume—the more you ask, the more you could get confused. At a certain point you will need coffee grounds at the perfume counter to bring you back to olfactory neutrality. Put the issue to rest.

Stop asking. Surrender into Faith.

This confusion from asking too many questions has happened to me, and really it's just another way of overthinking. At some point I have to ground myself back to my initial intentions and focus on something else. My food, my tea, the sun, the sea. I think about me, but not the me that requires an answer. The Me that already has those things I've asked for. The wishes I asked to be granted. And I accept that they will soon be a part of my life, in whichever form they need to come, quietly and humbly, for the greater good.

Despite that pang to keep asking, to pull a card, call a friend, I now know to stop focusing on the thing I do not have an answer for. I have to remind myself that I have enough to keep me going right now. Not focusing on the situation gives space to explore other aspects of my life in the now and less time to worry.

Faith is easier when you know that thing you're manifesting is already yours, finding its way to you.

Trust that what you've asked for is locked in. Someone is doing the magic for you. Worry about nothing but showing up as your best Self, every day.

Visualization

> *To bring anything into your life, imagine that it's already there.*
> **RICHARD BACH**

Two years ago, I visualized living in a nice apartment in a big city with a beautiful balcony from which I was looking down in full admiration of what I had accomplished to be there.

One year later, I was living in the apartment of my dreams, in a big city with a beautiful balcony from which I was looking down in full admiration of what I had accomplished to be there.

This is one of many examples. I never would've believed the power of visualization had this not happened to me.

Visualization works well when you imagine a desired outcome using as many senses as you can, so that your body, mind, and frequency can lock it in to attract it. Perhaps you may have seen a video or two, followed someone on Instagram, or spoken with a crypto trader about how they visualized their wealth?

At first I found it silly — quite ridiculous, really. What am I going to do? Sit here and picture myself driving a Ferrari with caviar spilling from my purse while imported champagne is misting the air, miraculously not damaging my perfectly coiffed hair? And then what? It just comes true? Okay.

> *Proper visualization by the exercise of concentration and willpower enables us to materialize thoughts, not only as dreams or visions in the mental realm but also as experiences in the material realm.*
>
> **PARAMAHANSA YOGANANDA**

I once attended a personal development program in Rome, led by Leonardo Leone, a clever Italian entrepreneur with a Tony Robbins-esque fervor mixed with elements of Neuro-linguistic Programming (NLP). It's a beautiful thing that he has brought these mental hacks and open ways of thinking to the Italian people and I do not regret the time I spent following his program.

So there I was, in my chair after a long day of learning about the mind, its limiting beliefs, how to succeed financially, and a variety of alternative interpretations of society. Then it came time to do a visualization. I had just broken up with my ex and was living in the apartment we had shared in a tiny little town in Italy, with a deep inner knowing that if I didn't soon leave that town, I'd fossilize with the rest of the relics in the ceramics museum it was known for.

How, though? I had €87 in my bank account at the time I was doing this exercise. I wasn't *that* poor, but I had mistakenly transferred more money to my US account than I should have. In any case, it was particularly ironic as we sat there affirming *I am rich, I am financially abundant, I have everything, more than what I need, my wallet is overflowing.*

But also, what did I have to lose?

> *The clearer you are when visualizing your dreams, the brighter the spotlight will be to lead you on the right path.*
> **GAIL LYNNE GOODWIN**

We went for it. Surround-sound music, low lights, tears flowing, crowd cheering, everyone in the audience was living the dreams in their mind and so was I. It was a very potent mix of Ludovico Einaudi and our conscious intentions. I visualized my emotions, my sense of achievement, what I was wearing (a long, black dress with a turtleneck and diamond necklace), and what I was doing—hosting friends, pouring champagne, taking pictures, and later, looking out my balcony and smiling, feeling so grateful for all that had led me there.

And yes, it took about a year, almost long enough for me to have forgotten about it. I lived my life, Covid started, I began my journey of meditation and healing, and one year later I found the apartment I had imagined for myself in Milan. It wasn't until after I had moved in, after I poured champagne for a couple of friends who had stopped by and we posed for pictures, that I went to my balcony and remembered. This is exactly what I asked for. And I was proud and grateful for all that had led me there.

> *When you visualize for the joy of visualizing rather than with the intention of correcting some deficiency, your thoughts are more pure and therefore more powerful.*
>
> **ABRAHAM HICKS**

You can visualize anything you want, and as long as it is in alignment with your higher purpose, the coast is clear! Or, at least, clear to be cleared! However, it may or may not work if you visualize something that might not be in alignment with your higher purpose, or you are not yet so connected to that channel—for example: *I want to be so rich that I am swimming in a sea of money without ever having to do anything.* Sounds boring to me, but you can try it!

I've practiced more visualizations since then, including mini ones like "I am ready to receive the funding I need to carry forth my projects now," only to meet someone the next day whose job is to find projects to fund.

> *The key to effective visualization is to create the most detailed, clear and vivid a picture to focus on as possible. The more vivid the visualization, the more likely, and quickly, you are to begin attracting the things that help you achieve what you want to get done.*
>
> **GEORGE ST-PIERRE**

Here is the main idea behind a good visualization: you want to experience it on as many levels as you can across the senses, including the emotional, auditive, and physical.

Suggested visualization steps:

1. Put on some good music that is positive, energetic, and motivating.
2. Get into the mood of how you will feel during a climactic moment of victory. Are you happy, proud, excited, energized? Start to feel this way. As if you already had it.
3. You can add a physical stimulus, like the water washing over you in the shower.
4. Visualize what you'll be doing the moment you achieve what you're visualizing. Maybe you're feeling the feelings, imagining who's around you, what they're saying, what you'll be wearing, where you'll be, the weather, the view, the time of year. Don't rush it; wait until it feels real.
5. Speak out loud the words you'll be telling yourself when you get there.
6. Now go a bit further—imagine some time has passed and things are *even better* than what you expected. What does that look like for you? How do you feel now?
7. Repeat step 4. Don't rush it; wait until it feels real.
8. Lock in your visualization by doing a celebratory dance, feeling all the emotions, all the joy, all the excitement, all the gratitude.
9. Thank the Universe for allowing you to access this moment in time, so it is, and release it.

There you have it! Now let it go, let it flow, make good choices and be swift, confident, and proactive when the right things come your way. Make peace with your present, but keep on moving.

Be prepared to receive and aware that you can handle your own greatness. Your visualization is on its way. Be willing to do what it takes to make it happen.

> *Visualize the most amazing life imaginable to you. Close your eyes and see it clearly. Then hold the vision for as long as you can. Now place the vision in God's hands and consider it done.*
> **MARIANNE WILLIAMSON**

Gratitude

> *Acknowledging the good that you already have in your life is the foundation for all abundance.*
> **ECKHART TOLLE**

Being in a state of gratitude is by far the most important pre-qualifier for manifesting blessings into your life. If the Universe is serving lunch, would it bring a free dessert to the person complaining or to the person who is grateful? What you appreciate appreciates you back. And furthermore, outside of time and space what you are seeking is already with you, so feeling the gratitude of having it is another step towards receiving it faster.

Feeling grateful is a state of mind that you can practice daily, even if gratitude doesn't happen naturally at first. Many of us have so much going for us, but we focus on what we are lacking instead of what we have. So if you're reading this and you have a job, citizenship, a place to live, food on your table, friends and family you love and who support you, then any of those alone is reason enough to be grateful.

As you gear up for the day with your morning coffee, take a conscious pause to admire where you are and who you are today, and experience that feeling of gratitude. Do this anytime, whether it be walking around your house feeling how lucky you are to live there, or when you're out and about having an experience. You can also blatantly declare your gratitude out loud by repeating "Thank You" as many times as you can for a minute or two when you wake up in the morning or go to sleep at night. Stating words out loud reinforces the vibration and can be a powerful propeller towards achieving your higher purpose.

> *We create our life every day. Every thought process shapes our life. Positivity, gratitude and abundance in thoughts gives us power to manifest our dream life.*
> **PURVI RANIGA**

Without feeling grateful, is anything really worthwhile? As Jenifer Lewis once said, you have to be happy on your way to happy. So it is with gratitude. And don't we all want to achieve something we are deeply grateful for? Might as well feel it regardless of what you want beyond this moment.

What sense is there in receiving something incredible if you aren't going to enjoy it? How can you receive something awesome if you aren't connected to the frequency of awesomeness? Connecting to the frequency of awesomeness means feeling abundant, and feeling abundant means your cup is overflowing, and when your cup is overflowing, you are grateful because you have everything you need and more.

BEING REAL

It's not about being holy or enlightened and all that stuff. It's about being real… Real when you are in the light but also when in the darkness.

MAESTRO YAKU QUAYLA

The realms of your authentic expression are a place to play in and explore.

Imagine you have just one hour left on this Earth, and it takes you half an hour to do the last thing you need to do before you die.

Are you going to sit there and listen to that PowerPoint, drowning in meaningless jabber?

Would you give the homeless person €20?

Find within you the power to live your life in a direct and transparent way. Be consistent and direct with who you always would be if you had one hour left. Own your darkness, own your light.

When we can sense we have a limited time left, the fire and vigor of urgency seep through our veins. Clarity! A renewed spirit of action!

We can choose our reactions, but it's not efficient to remain on our high horse for too long, contemplating that which feels most noble. There is no need to spend time overthinking and compromising our gut reactions in an effort to constantly exemplify wisdom; we can just be a person. A person who has had a change of thought, a new realization. Energy shifts quickly. You can be embarrassed, you can be hurt, you can feel passion, you can be anything in the plethora of feelings that are available to us, just don't make your feelings somebody else's issue. Neutralize. Be in your own truth, and follow where it takes you.

The Universe wants to help you achieve your goals and conspires to do so more easily if you are being real with yourself and others. When you are real, you spare yourself the hassle of burying issues that later need to be dug out and dealt with. You save time by acting in accordance with your values (which only your conscience can discern), and may the pieces fall from there! If something falls through, you are only making room for something else in the end.

When someone asks you for a favor and you don't feel like doing it, it's okay to say no. And it's okay to feel some type of way when something upsets you. In fact, it's important to acknowledge the triggering feeling to prevent it from tethering itself to you. The further you go on your journey, well beyond this book, the less things will rattle you. But stay human. Let yourself feel. Sprinkle some pepper and lime into your guacamole.

It is just as ineffective to be passive and resentful, disguised as loving and kind, as it is to be flat out aggressive and condescending.

We choose how to direct our energy, always. When things feel unbalanced or something seems off, be real. Clear it away. And when something is cool, be open. Enjoy it wholeheartedly. Find your power, roar your truth. Rely on yourself to navigate that moment rather than relying on time, or on fate, or on how a specific person may or may not react. Those things are happening anyway.

You don't need to be like anybody else to become somebody great.
You need to be 100% yourself and succeed in your own skin.

GEOFFREY OCAYA

Choose the actions and reactions that set you free. Don't be rude, be real. As Quayla also once said, we are imperfect beings in an imperfect world, and that is mathematically perfect. Just be.

You Don't Have Time

You don't have time to be anyone but yourself.

You truly do not have time to be anyone but yourself.

Be Fully In

> *Unless commitment is made, there are only promises and hopes; but no plans.*
> **PETER DRUCKER**

A warrior has no time to worry about the outcome of his death, he lives in the present moment. And in that moment, he is absolutely and completely present. One must be fearlessly committed, like a warrior.

What did it take for the warrior to be in that state of mind? At some point in his life he understood his purpose was to become a warrior. He trained for it and embodied a mindset that included this image in his identity. He understood the implications on his life and decided to go for it. The risk was worth taking. When called into battle, he was aware he may not come out alive, and that this was the destiny he created.

Would you die for your purpose? Sounds like an extreme question, but it's not so far from where you need to be when making a decision about your life's direction.

To be fully in is to be committed. I will use these terms interchangeably.

Commitment sends a very powerful message to the Universe. Unless we commit to something and take a firm stance on where we want our lives to go, we are dilly-dallying through possibilities that each seem fine, but have no single finish line. A path is only a path. When we do not choose what path we're on, it becomes frustrating in the long term. Indecision is a form of suffering; not knowing what to commit to is particularly hard for Souls who know they have something deep and wonderful to let out — which is in all of us.

I have met talented and beautiful individuals who are lost today because they never fully committed to finding themselves and growing towards their purpose. Fascinating people with such potential who repeatedly chose the path that kept their options most open, and their fears most at bay. Thinking they had time. Later blaming external circumstances for why things didn't work out, not ever realizing this blame prevented them from achieving happiness all along.

Being fully in means fighting your demons until you love them enough that they recognize who they are dealing with. It means having conviction above all others that this is the path you are going to take. It means *HELL YES!* to a path *and I don't need anyone to endorse it.* Through sickness and health, for richer or poorer, I am marrying this path. When you commit, you hope for the best and you take every risk that comes with it, accepting the eventuality of letting go of whatever is not congruent with that path.

Sometimes we fear greatness because deep in the least explored caverns of our psyches we know we will lose people in our lives, people who won't resonate with the person we are meant to blossom into. Other times we don't think we deserve it. Or we don't have a track record or example of succeeding, so we lack the confidence to believe success is possible. We may feel cozy and comfortable at home but unable to take risks.

Other times we approach going into greatness the wrong way because we feel entitled and demanding of it, without understanding the magnitude of preparation and responsibility that comes with choosing a path. We don't yet understand the humility required to maintain success as well as peace within. When we ask for greatness with entitlement, our Soul will know we are cheating and either not give it to us or it will come with a price. Perhaps we will achieve monetary gain but suffer in other ways.

Know yourself. Learn to like and love yourself today, as you are. Work on the aspects that make you feel worthy of embracing all the good that could come from achieving a great outcome — while remaining aware of any blind spots.

> *Do the thing and you will be given the power.*
> **RALPH WALDO EMERSON**

Find it, be it, do it. Be fully in.

Receiving

> *Opportunity doesn't make appointments, you have to be ready when it arrives.*
> **TIM FARGO**

When you invite a guest to stay with you, you clean your house, you buy snacks, you make sure to have clean sheets. You get You (mentally) and your house (physically) ready to welcome the guest. In the same way one prepares their house to receive a visitor, one must prepare themSelves to receive in life.

We all get hints from the Universe of what our best path is, including what decisions reflect our truest Selves on our way to receiving that with which we need to align. Some choose to listen, others cannot hear so well, and others prefer to stay the same. We always have free choice.

But the people who time and time again choose to go towards their light, who are willing to make difficult choices in honor of that path, receive the quickest and best support from the Universe.

We must remember that somewhere out there and within us is a space that holds us. A space for us to express ourSelves without judgment. A space that doesn't care when or how you do something. This space holds all the outcomes that are possible to You. And to unlock the magic formula, all it takes is knowing what you want, being ready for it, and vibing right to receive it.

> *Giving and receiving are different expressions of the same flow of Energy in the Universe.*
> **DEEPAK CHOPRA**

Perhaps you have some blocks to expose and transform along the way. Maybe they're financial blocks, maybe they're emotional. Don't be afraid, we all have blocks. Go back to a place of abundance. Lead with love, not fear. The best thing of all is having the opportunity to give, to tip well if it feels good and you have the means, pay for someone's dinner, help a homeless person… Whenever these things happen, you are giving and therefore getting a fresh chance to receive something new. Giving starts the receiving process; one calls forth the other.

When you are ready, it will happen. Remember: You call for it to come. The Universe has a funny way of answering. Whether it be through people, or rewards, or moments, or places, the Universe knows exactly the right time to bring them to your plate for the taking, but only when you are ready to experience and comprehend the power that comes with giving and receiving. You must feel worthy, and remain humble, of being able to hold the space when that power comes in.

It gets easier and easier to receive. Once you receive something from this pure and direct channel, the floodgates open. Just like when you learn to love yourself and find inner peace, nobody can take that away from you. In this way, you learn what it means to receive. And it becomes easier and easier to enter that state once you have activated that knowledge. Activation is an anchor you can go back to over and over again. You have found the light switch and lit a new lightbulb within your chandelier of working with the energies of the Universe.

PART 4

ROMANTIC RELATIONSHIPS

SECTION INTRODUCTION

How many things there are which I do not want.
SOCRATES

I need to come clean.

I've certainly had my fair share of relationships that were successful in their own right, at their own time, only for them to eventually end. But I did not yet love myself enough to take on a lifetime of loving someone. Now I have found the path to myself (or the path to determine the path), cleared the blocks, and learned how nice it is to receive through self-love first. Without these experiences, I would still be attracting the same lessons over and over. Unless we have achieved alignment within ourselves, no relationship can be a good one.

An important ingredient to relationships is trust. Prepping for a relationship is also about trust—Trust in ourselves, in the work we've done to better ourselves, and in our ability to recognize when the right person comes our way. Trusting that we are at our best and reflecting that vibration in whom we attract. Sometimes trust means deciding that you are ready for something serious if you have not been attracted to stability and consistency before.

Trusting is by far the best way to start anything off and relax about it. Making trust your vibration is the first step towards attracting and finding someone who is on your frequency.

Life is really ours to grab and delight in. Everything we come across is inspiration and preparation for our future Selves, so we must be curious about what happens to us in life. We must be inspired to think differently, experience differently, learn about ourselves, and see the humor in things. We must notice when our own behaviors and patterns are getting triggered and coming out, understanding that every situation is preparation for something great to come.

We always have free will in the divine timing of our life, but there is also a greater plan. A path of least resistance and highest growth. What makes the difference between snail moves and Formula-One-level growth is consciousness — the ability to switch gears and go faster through our awareness. The faster we figure out the story behind a situation, the faster that situation is understood, neutralized, and overcome.

As you continue your journey to find love, look for the signs. A little feather on the sidewalk, a text at just the right moment, an encouraging message on a billboard you happen to be walking by. Live your life, continue to fulfill yourSelf, and stay in tune with the life surrounding you.

One more thing before we dive in. Below is a timeline for each phase of the romantic relationships we will be covering. Sometimes dating can span a number of months with no established exclusivity, and sometimes things can progress into partnership on a clearer and faster timeline. In any case, time can be a bit of an illusion. The events that take place follow more of an established order.

DATING	EARLY TOGETHERNESS	PARTNERSHIP
(from early meeting, up to "the talk")	(after dating, exclusivity is established)	(a serious, established relationship)

CHAPTER 7

DATING

Life is a long pilgrimage from fear to love.
PAULO COELHO

Ah, l'amour. So beautiful and unpredictable. Painful, scary, daunting. But *somehow*, no matter how hurt we get, it's the one thing we are always willing to put ourselves out there for. It's wired within us to continue seeking companionship, it's what we are here for: to spread and receive love. There are just way too many benefits when it goes well!

Dating is *not* for the faint of heart. You've got to put yourself out there and get vulnerable. It can be raw and embarrassing. Maybe you overshare, overtext, or do something "irreversible." You may discover that your enthusiasm is not a match for another person's fear of commitment or your desire to wait to get under the sheets could offend another person's ego.

You could regret saying something and regret not saying something. You might feel so seen, understood, and enchanted that you open up, only to realize that that person did not have the capacity to hold the space for you in the long term.

Goodness knows all of these things can happen. And I have seen highly spiritually evolved people fall for these human dating traps, because dating is really, really human.

Unlike forced relationships, there is no such thing as doing the wrong thing when a person is meant to be in your life. You enter your own dance where you both suddenly know the moves and are not threatened by one another's moves. What they do is perfectly reciprocal to what you do, and if it's not, it's complementary. Regardless, it feels comfortable. It feels safe.

There are tricks you can adopt in order to safeguard and prepare for a successful dating venture, minimizing embarrassment and maximizing clarity. First, you shouldn't get attached to anyone until you feel confident that there is a mutually demonstrated consistency. Hold your horses, because something great will wait, whether or not you jump in headfirst. So let's explore together.

STARTING SOMETHING NEW

What do you like about them? Besides pulse, respiration, and body parts?
CAROLYN HAX

Whether we are happily coupled, happily single, or, of course, dating, most of us can relate to the uncertainties in the beginning of a relationship. The beginning phase can be downright frightening, maybe even slightly embarrassing if you are both too shy to admit that you like each other.

If you meet organically (as in, not through a dating app), your relationship could start from a real-life crush.

Getting a crush is fun!

It's like that person is just reachable enough, but you can't be sure you'll ever have them.

Until you think you might. It's giddiness and shyness at the same time. Like when you're in the middle of recess at school and a friend tells you someone might like you. Your hearing suddenly gets really sharp and you can hear what that new crush is saying from across the room while three different conversations are happening around you. You can feel them looking at you, you dissect their body language. Are their knees pointing towards you? Did they hear *you* say that thing in group conversation that was meant only for them to hear?

You want more of them, but you're afraid of any further interaction. It's adorable.

So. That's a crush.

But say you've met on a dating app, where the first date is much more clearly outlined. It's an agreed-upon event where we all know the framework.

The first date is easy, to an extent. We show up, and ideally we can live in the moment. With refreshingly few expectations and a nice appreciation for one another if it goes well. The more feminine energy allows the masculine energy to start things off and initiate further texting and date planning while she receives and responds to it.

After the second or third date some of the misunderstandings might begin. That's the first moment many '"situationships" tend to drop off.

Around the second and third date, if you so choose it, sex has a big impact on the misunderstandings. It is around this time that two well-intentioned people begin to project some of their expectations onto each other. This is a crucial make-or-break-it moment. One could become more anxious, one more direct or avoidant. Each still doing their best, if they like the person, to "play it cool."

Around the third date mark, an unknown tension in how we communicate our needs and wants might start happening. It's tricky because neither person owes the other anything, but this unknown tension is a phase of getting to know each other and allowing each other the space to continue to expand.

It's one thing to say we want to play the dance of disclosure and mystery and another to do it, of course. Unhealed triggers and traumas always find a way to, well, get triggered.

Have you ever caught yourself sending a risky text to the person you really like because you crave the same attention you had when you were together? But you send the text right when they are needing some space?

Goodness forbid we send a double text (a text later in the day without a response to the first), a longer than usual paragraph, or a goodnight text with a heart emoji. And when that person doesn't react in the way we had expected, we no longer feel safe or in our power. Maybe all we get back is a brief emoji. Or maybe we get no response for hours.

And rather than feeling into the discomfort, not attaching ourselves to the outcome, and allowing that person to be completely free in their reactions (just as we are), we might draw conclusions instead of giving them the benefit of the doubt. Maybe the other person truly is this way and they've tried their well-meaning best to keep up this far in your interactions.

Sometimes we spiral, desperately feeling a need to end the uncertainty within, assuming the worst and sabotaging ourselves rather than giving the benefit of doubt, taking time to understand ourselves and speaking up from a graceful space.

We think to ourselves, *That's it. Now I won't message first for at least three or four times. Let's see what they do to regain my interest. That'll wake them up.*

We might shift to indirect, manipulative, and passive-aggressive responses, waiting for we don't know *what* to happen next. All of these unnecessary games so we can feel safe again in what should be the easiest and most beautiful state of being.

Love. Honesty. Vulnerability. Confidence. That's the real game.

What would happen if we just felt the feelings we needed to feel without externalizing or judging our pain? What if we released our attachment to the other person and saw that the story is on us, without the expectation of anything in return? It's a difficult practice, but doing this would allow us to feel okay with any outcome. It would inject lightness back into the intensity. It would create space for that person to show up in the way they wanted, and it would give the relationship a good, honest shot from the start.

Let's dial it back now and start with who we are attracting in the first place.

Attraction

> *Attraction is beyond our will or ideas sometimes.*
> **JULIET BINOCHE**

Attraction is alluring and complex. It's an indispensable trait, but if that is the only thing you are focusing on you'll be blinded, and stray far away from your truth.

We attract what we are ready for.

If we are in a place of chaos and emotional confusion, we will attract people who have similar challenges. Or we may have evolved to a great place, but life still tests us with a person who is battling the very demons we just fought! How interesting! Can you handle it? Do you want to? It's yours to decide. As you continue to evolve and pick up new stimuli from others, your energetic state can be highly influenced from one instant to the next! Notice who you are meeting, and what state you are in.

> *The law of attraction states that like attracts like, and when you think and feel what you want to attract on the inside, the law will use people, circumstances or events to magnetize what you want.*
> **RHONDA BYRNE**

There's nothing wrong with being attracted to someone who exhibits the unhealthy traits from a past relationship — this happens. Things that are bad for us are really, really attractive sometimes. And repeating lessons are meant to happen, to varying degrees, like fast-tracked final quizzes. But it's not until we find a way to pass the class that we've truly learned the lesson.

The people we are most attracted to, particularly in an unbalanced and difficult-to-control way, are there to teach us lessons.

If we haven't cleared our slate, our history can certainly play a role in who we attract. Until we break the patterns, unpeel the layers, and learn to know who we are deep inside, we can become attracted to people who aren't great for us because they offer us a familiar wound or an unfamiliar one (in both cases, no balance). We gravitate towards these people because we are subconsciously looking to resolve unresolved traumas or evade those traumas through the other person. Our subconscious tells us, if you fix this person, you've fixed your childhood as well. Fun trick: If you find yourself in such a situation, ask, *With which parent did I have to fight the most in order to be loved, and what person did I need to be in order to receive that love? Am I being them now? Are they?*

Look. Sometimes our path is simple and we meet a person who is meant to accompany us through a series of lessons, perhaps even life. For those who marry young or stay together from a very young age, that's a remarkable story. But if this doesn't happen, there's no need to be upset.

Learning to appreciate the closed doors allows many more to open. NO simply means Next Opportunity. You must fully close the door, and only you can fully know that you did. If you don't fully close it, guess what? You'll attract people who also didn't close their doors and find yourself in a *menage à quatre or even a menage à cinq* (i.e. dating someone who is also stringing along other people) with scattered hopes and dreams, leftover energies bleeding into the beginning of what could have been a clean start to a beautiful story. Anything is possible, and if it's meant to be it will be — but why attract difficult stories?

Sometimes we are attracted to a person and at the same time feel undeserving of them. Being able to have them feels improbable, which fuels the attraction further, like we are graced by their fleeting presence. Take note of these micro feelings. Would that person actually be there for you when you needed them?

> *There's always a common attraction to universal needs of love and a feeling of worthiness.*
> **MORAN ATIAS**

You are just as wonderful as the person you are attracted to and worthy of receiving their attention. If that person picked you, you are worthy of them — always remember that. Never forget how great you are as you bask in the greatness of the other.

When you feel like you are going down a regressive spiral, just notice. Notice your attention has gravitated towards this one person, and what it is doing to you. This person may be good for you or bad for you (though, of course, no one is truly bad for you unless it is physical abuse, because everyone teaches a lesson). You are just noticing you like them. You don't know yet how the situation will unfold. It might end there. It could simply be having a flirty exchange with the bank teller at the counter, and that's it.

Say we get to a place where the attraction can go further and we've decided to pursue it. We've even indulged in being with this person, shared a kiss, or more. When we are young or if we aren't careful even as adults, it can overwhelm us as we get dazed, which prevents us from seeing things rationally.

This is why it's important to have a true understanding of who we are and an awareness that this could take place. And be especially aware that bringing sex into the mix can be super fun and, even more, super-duper confusing because it's very hormonal. Our goal should be to not lose ourselves completely, so we need to be aware of the dangers of our own self-sabotaging mind, which does its best but it's layers have created unnecessary rules to protect us.

The more we know ourSelves, the more we can also identify when we are losing ourSelves, and recognize it's time to recalibrate.

How do we recalibrate? Let's review. We take space! Space to be with our Selves and nourish ourselves back to wholeness with our own energy. Because with everyone we meet, there is an energy exchange. And even when we meet the right person for us, there are moments of elation, bliss, and perhaps some disequilibrium triggered by biology. Our hormones can go crazy around that person because our primordial brains are telling us to reproduce!

But if we've built a life we love, a routine that we enjoy, and daily reminders of who we are…then we have that to go back to, to ground ourSelves, to cut through the intensity. It also gives a break to the other person, who might otherwise feel, on an energetic level, that you're constantly obsessing over them — and it restores the lightness back to the relationship.

By remaining self-reliant, confident, and satisfied with your life's mission and accomplishments, and remaining whole within, you can spot the triggers that are taking you off balance.

Attraction, in and of itself, can be fun, of course! Roller coasters are enjoyable when we know we are on one. But we mustn't let go of who we are and get dragged into the identity of someone else. We should hold onto our goals, dreams, aspirations, and long-term rewards.

You may be attracted to someone now, and you may not know what to do with yourself. With all this energy and desire to check out of life, you allow yourself to dream about your idealized future with that person, melting into their identity like a caramel sugar candy in the pan.

Just allow it for a bit, experience it to the degree that you can't avoid it, and then gently bring yourself back to Earth. Living in the future of unfulfilled and unguaranteed expectations is a recipe for suffering.

Take a deep breath and remind yourself of who you are. It is great that you met, but always remember who you are.

Simple, right? Knowledge is power. And you can forgive yourself in advance if you need to learn this lesson a few times in life. People can take us by surprise, they can take us off balance with their unique list of qualities that generate intense attraction. The heart often wants to rationalize a good story or a romantic beginning, neglecting other warning signs that come its way.

Whether this is the right person for you or the wrong person for you, allow it to unfold. If at any moment things need to be interrupted, that's okay. Stay in your truth. Accept when you fall off balance, allow it to sit with you, and remember how deserving you are of a great outcome.

Look up at the sky, watch the sun or the stars and put your hand on your heart. Say it out loud: "I am ready to give and receive unconditional love and I am ready for the greatest love of my life." Or anything else you'd like to call in, irrespective of the person you are currently seeing.

And instead of sending an unprompted text if you're feeling angsty, sit still for a few breaths, close your eyes, and begin to release your thoughts. Because if it's not *that* person, it's going to be another. There's always another. Worry about growing firmly into yourSelf. Are you achieving your goals? Do you have a passion? Thank the Universe for bringing you to where you are today, for every moment that brought you here, and for allowing you to experience the highs and lows that come with the amazing start of what could be a wonderful relationship with someone new…but *always* with yourSelf first.

Passion

> *Love without passion is dreary; passion without love is horrific.*
> **LORD BYRON**

The flames, the touching, the fire burning in your pants. Passion: a highly criticized attribute, where you're damned if you do and damned if you don't.

Passion comes down to personal tolerance, really. If you can do with less of it, you're likely better off and more able to determine the viability of the rapport. If you value the physical aspect in a relationship, then passion is indispensable for you, so it would behoove you to learn to weave with its power in the beginning.

Understanding one another's intentions is as important as nudity and body enchantment.

There's usually one partner who is more exuberant than the other. It's up to the partner that recognizes this to understand whether they are comfortable keeping up or whether they want to take it down a notch.

As difficult as it was to fight the temptation, I've never regretted taking things slow in a relationship, particularly when I felt the passion to be strong. Anyone who stuck around was well worth keeping.

It is my humble observation that emotional passion is a precursor to good sex. However, as the quote at the beginning of this chapter states, things can quickly become out of control when you give precedence to steamy physicality without having gotten to know the person apart from the hormones.

You might be thinking, *What if I spend months getting to know a person and developing genuine feelings, only to later discover things aren't clicking in the bedroom?* If this happens, you may end up trying to convince yourself things are fine and will improve, wasting more time making sense of where you've ended up, rationalizing the good against the bad. Sex therapist Barry McCarthy found that when sex was good in a relationship, it accounted for about ten to fifteen percent of overall satisfaction, but when sex was a challenge or lacking altogether, it accounted for about forty to fifty percent of the couple's satisfaction. We want to avoid this, clearly.

What happens scientifically in the classic example of doing it right away? It's passion, one might say! It's romantic, artistic, *French*. But what is it about this scenario that often (not always) leads one partner to disappear, despite the extremely satisfying experience? Differing expectations. And because the energy can shift for one person very quickly, the other can become insecure and feel guilty they did something "out of character" such as sex on the first date, at the very moment where confidence would be better suited. To anyone currently reading this, if you're feeling regretful about sleeping with someone too soon because now they are cooling off, the worst thing you can do is tell the person this is how you feel. Own it and be proud of that decision!

So, this section sounded like it was going to be fun, and yet here we are talking about the aftermath of putting passion first. We need to proceed with awareness of our hearts, our energy, and our ability to remain sovereign. Then we can take the knowledge of our own humanity into account. Once again, the journey always leads back to us. Honoring ourSelves is the most important component of any big decision, and that includes being aware of what does or does not lead us into sharing our bodies.

Of course, there are times when we aren't expecting a single thing from a person and we manage to fall into a wonderful partnership where the passion is strong, both people feel free, and no one holds back from anything physical from the start. This happens too! The trick is not to attach to any outcome, to experience the moment *in* the moment without expecting a single thing, other than a continued appreciation of the moment together — this makes room for fun surprises that turn into the future.

Sex

> *Sexual intimacy is a continuing process of discovery.*
> **SHERI STRITOF**

Sex is an evolution. And if we've had more than one partner throughout our lives, sex becomes primarily a relationship with ourSelves and our bodies that unfolds over time, before we share it forever with someone else. When we are young or when we first have sex, we have no idea what we are doing. And to anyone who isn't experienced in this department, take those moments to learn what you truly like and what works for you when you are in the act. Learn it for yourself, so that you can recreate it with that same person or with someone new.

It's like riding a bike or skiing. First you need to learn how the mechanism works, and more importantly how it works with your beautiful body. Once you learn it, you can ride your bike or ski down any mountain, so enjoy it!

Sex is a beautiful invitation to live in the moment with another body (or more!) next to yours. Our bodies are designed to make us feel super good when we are together! We shouldn't take this away from ourselves. It's a natural, incredible healing process to be able to share yourself physically with someone. It's even more incredible to have that energy build up over time where two people see the value in exploring each other, for themselves, for the other person, and for the relationship across an unforeseen future.

Sex is also an energy exchange. So we need to be careful of not depleting our own carefully and lovingly curated energy. Not everyone should be entitled to access our energy, unless we are willing to empty our tanks for anyone that comes across it. It's good to be selective about who we share our energy with. This doesn't mean waiting three months because a book told you so, or having other conditions around sex. You do it when you feel good about it, with no explicit agenda behind it. When you feel safe with the energy of the other person, when you feel you can both handle the amazing thing you are about to do together and can honor each other for it.

When two people are evolved about what sex can be, when they are honest, straightforward, and unashamed of who they are in the act, that's when the real fun happens (as long as nobody is getting hurt, of course). It's fun because nobody knows what it can become, but it can become exciting. Are you ready to hear what the ingredients are? Being in the moment. Breathing together. Not being embarrassed. Accepting that both people have a background and are allowed to appreciate sex. On a side note, all these things become enhanced once we practice meditation and mental foreplay.

Sex can also be abominably awkward and awful. There are people who never discover their sexuality or they discover it too late and get stuck in ruts of compromise because the relationship outside sex is giving them enough. A peaceful homelife, a stable, mutual understanding, everything else "works." And for some people, sex isn't even that important!

But we are talking about feeling fulfilled in every way in a relationship, and that means sex, too. That means sex is important. Sex is the only thing that distinguishes your relationship from a friendship. So, decide how good you want it to be and how important it is to you.

Whatever your body enjoys, you should find someone that equally embraces it with similar frequency. That's the only way to have a satisfying life with someone in which one person doesn't have to compromise and resent the other (as can happen in all too many cases).

Most importantly, remember that it's always healthy to love our bodies and to develop a pleasing relationship with our bodies. Connecting with ourselves is healthy, calming, and lovely.

EARLY COMPLICATIONS OF DATING

It is better to understand little than to misunderstand a lot.
ANATOLE FRANCE

Within the delicate dance of dating are many slippery moments, and these are the hardships we tend to hold onto and gossip about to our friends. The missed calls, the triple texts, the incomprehensible behaviors. The love bombing, the who-pays-for-what confusion, the ghosting, the scary feelings, all of these things can happen in early dating.

Should anything come up, like new reactions and confusing behaviors, I invite you to figure out which parts have come from you and which ones are coming from the other person. If two people are aligned within themselves and what they want, they will remain on a baseline of trust and understanding with one another despite human, situational hurdles. Trusting yourSelf is all you need. You have the wisdom.

Let's dive into the hypothetical of a real, early dating dilemma that someone once shared with me. As tends to happen more and more in our interconnected world, you have found each other through social media and have quickly started daily correspondence over the phone. You message regularly, beginning with a seven o'clock morning text all the way to a nighttime goodnight without even knowing each other in person yet.

Since you don't live in the same country, you decide to meet soon in a city midway between you. There is one little material distinction between the two of you. The other person is significantly more well off at this stage in their career. As you begin planning, it is unclear who will be paying for the accommodation. It seemed they had volunteered to, based on how they led the situation, but you are now at a standstill at the stage of booking the hotel. They are taking no action to book. Days go by where you maintain regular correspondence and skirt around the subject. You wonder, *Should I just book the place myself?* That seems like the easiest way to end the agony of the unknown. But muted self-expression and possible resentment don't quite create a healthy pattern for the future. Outside of this block you continue communicating daily.

Caught in a place of waiting and not knowing, you notice the block itself. A block in communication, a resistance towards opening up enough to even discuss it. What is a highly developed connection in certain aspects is extremely underdeveloped in other aspects. However, by this point you feel invested in them, wanting to justify the effort you've both put forth to get to this place to begin with.

This justification process happens all the time in other ways, by the way. For instance, two people begin getting to know each other and start off on a good path of transparency. But if something falls off track, it seems easier to focus on the good and hope for that awkward moment to pass.

Rather than taking action to relieve the uncertainty by booking the ticket yourself, the best thing to do in these moments is to unplug from the situation, understand what is blocking you from expressing yourself, and come back neutrally with clarity and direction. This process allows for asking a non-charged question, such as, "Did we want to book the accommodation today? And how should we handle the payment?" Be okay with any scenario and response; there was an implication, but nobody owes anyone anything.

When we embody the calm, self-assured reality we have within, things are simple. Someone receives and someone gives. Then it switches.

That's the dance. Like a game of badminton — delicate, gentle swings of a gliding birdie into the air. Staying calm and in our place, we wait for the birdie to come to us, then we swing back.

In the beginning, despite having invested time, it's important to remain interested in how it's going to turn out without expecting a specific outcome. They didn't write back? Okay, that's interesting! Maybe write *them*. Or maybe they actually like you so much that they are grasping for balance — give space. Everything you do is okay, just think positive for you and choose the narrative that feels best (and realistic). Know yourSelf and the loving truth that is in you. Be willing to change if the relationship stops aligning with your highest growth path.

Everyone has blocks! Focus on the solution. You work on your process while they work on theirs. Allow each other to show up in your fullest powers. And if they are not working on themselves the way you are, the fact that you are working on yourself will still help evolve the situation. Then you can decide again and again if you are right for each other.

Sometimes letting go means being open to not being right and then coming together with greater understanding of yourSelf and consequently the other person. Do not be attached to an outcome, be attached to your mission, the mission of your highest Self. Let the other person show you who they are little by little. Notice if the dynamic takes you away from your highest expression or supports your growth. You can care for someone and at the same time recognize they are not right for you. Watch how the pieces fall.

Being Love Bombed

Ninety percent of true love is acute, ear-burning embarrassment.
TERRY PRATCHETT

It's hard to tell if you're experiencing the genuine enthusiasm of a spontaneous and exuberant person who is delighted to have met you and open to starting a relationship, or if you are, in fact, being love bombed by compliments and future projections of someone's idealistic, unrealistic future desires.

Love bombing occurs when someone demonstrates disproportionate interest in you at the beginning of courtship. Their interest is so extravagant that you begin to believe their feelings are true. In turn, your own real, loving feelings are activated, and you fall for them. As soon as you fall for them, they drop the proverbial "love" bomb on you and you remain completely kerfuffled.

If love bombing has happened to you before, you might have an idea it's happening again and be able to heed the warning. If that's the case for you, good riddance to the love bomber. Let's hope to have a healthy dose of caution and awareness in order to avoid it again, and high five to you for surviving that.

I personally did not recognize when I was being love bombed. In my story, I allowed myself to get swept away. At first, I did not particularly like him. But he was persistent and consistent. His charm was in his quickness to respond, his stoic demeanor, and, superficially, his body. After the first two months he wanted to give me his house keys, and soon after that, chemistry permitting, I felt I had fallen in love. I felt so bamboozled by his openness towards serious commitment that I decided to tell him I loved him. As soon as I did, the house of cards fell to the ground. He got scared, he needed time, I caught him with his ex and, of course, I folded shortly after.

What is the profile of a love bomber? They look like a person who isn't able to see the other person as they are but as someone who can help them create the illusion of an ideal relationship. Love bombing is a very under-studied subject, perhaps closely tied to narcissism, though not necessarily. While narcissists do not know who they are outside of external validation, a love bomber sees the other person as a means to an end, a way to complete their perfect image of a couple without truly seeing the person for who they are. They might get fixated on an idealized extreme they see in the other person. The love bombee will rightfully feel hesitant at first, like most people would feel when a relationship is moving so fast. Yet the confidence of the love bomber is reassuring, so as soon as the bombee starts feeling safe to be themselves and grows accustomed to being loved by the love bomber, that's when the tables turn and the turkey gravy is poured on their heads.

How to recognize the behavior of a love bomber?

If someone is suspiciously obsessed with you at first sight, or making quick promises about a future together, or trying to get you to go on a long trip early on, or stating what a missing puzzle piece you are in their lives — those are some clues. Although it's nice to believe in romance — and some of the most captivating love stories may start with 'I knew from the moment I saw them…" — science proves to us that only after a story has gone well do we remember things with those rose-colored lenses. A love bomber has absolutely no idea how that love is going to work out. They want to, but they don't. They are not prepared to discover you have flaws or sides of you that are human. It's not only conditional, it's delusional.

When a person challenges you to be a player in the game of their love life, this is also a red flag. They may say something like, "You might be the one who will change my heart" or "Let's see if I fall in love this year," and give you a *wink wink* over dinner. Then you might want to twist your eyebrow and think more closely at what is driving them to say this. Their words sound playful, but it's like someone telling you they are looking for someone else to solve their problem and disconnect from love.

Are they really available? And are you, in fact, *attracted* to a challenge, feeling safer knowing they aren't all in? Does it remind you of you? Does it activate within you the desire to conquer and earn love? Was there a time in your childhood when you had to fight for parental attention?

A love bomber is the opposite of cautious and aware. They charge straight ahead like a herd of wild animals not knowing what they are doing to you or themselves. Of course, they want something beautiful and loving from a relationship as well, but they are eons away from the awareness and presence that requires. There is a direct, positive correlation with how far away they are from their own self-awareness.

No one is strictly evil, and no one is strictly good. We have reactions to stimuli and we are responsible for how we choose to react. Each of those moments are constantly available to help us grow. Everyone can get there. Humanity is fluid and emotional maturity operates on a breadth of spectrums, like a dynamic continuum stretching across vast, unique places for two people to find each other and meet in the middle.

Love bombing isn't necessarily malicious, or narcissistic, or meant to trick you. A love bomber might simply be an emotionally unavailable person who doesn't realize their approach is not the way to go about the initial stages of love. In fact, they may be tricking themselves all along and end up suffering because of it, too. They don't feel so good either, once the tower of their expectations has fallen down.

Consistently doing the same thing, never questioning whether our behavior is the trigger, does not make us a bad person. It just makes us not so bright — just like you're not a bad person if you repeatedly bump your head against the wall and wonder why the wall turned out to be hard. It is, however, self-harm, and self-harm often involves casualties.

People who love bomb are magnets for lonely people who are thirsty for attention and unaware they are filling that void with someone else.

But life is more fun as a couple, you might say!

Correct! So make sure you are finding someone who is not going to take advantage of your readiness to start a relationship with their premature and overly-desirous imposition (which may or may not have anything to do with you). Whether they are aware or not, make sure they see you as your whole Self. And if they are not aware, be aware of them, for yourself.

If somehow you can navigate the bloated feelings in the beginning of a relationship — because perhaps life has nominated you the calmer one this time — and the other person *lets* you set the pace, then that's the whole key to making the relationship work.

Most of the time, though, when someone is love bombing you…you should run if you can. Or experience it if you can't help it. Hindsight is 20/20, as they say. There's a good lesson behind watching the castle burn before your very own eyes. If you are strong enough to try to set the pace and can't find a way to agree on that pace, do not stay in that relationship or waste your energy trying to be with someone who is stuck in a process that has nothing to do with you.

Look out for the ones who seek external validation. You are not responsible for completing anyone's idea of love or being anyone other than yourSelf.

Pulling Away

> *In its purest form, dating is auditioning for mating (and auditioning means we may or may not get the part).*
> **JOY BROWNE**

Sometimes you're on top of the world and sometimes you're wondering how you got to the bottom. When a new, untitled relationship begins to navigate its ebbs and flows, whether it's a symptom or a consequence, you or the other person could be starting to pull away. If you're the one taking distance and space, then there's no need for me to explain to you why you're doing it — simply look back on your triggers and traumas or notice the reasons for your dwindling attraction levels for that person. But if the person you're dating is the one pulling away, this section is for you.

Number one, here's what you do: you absolutely back off. Then ask yourself if you've been giving too much because it's what you were hoping to receive, and be honest with yourself if things no longer feel balanced because of it.

By now you understand this Self journey — or if you've chosen to start with the chapter on romantic relationships because you were impatient (I see you), hopefully you can first go back to reflect and see the value in confronting and understanding yourSelf better.

Whatever comes your way, accept it. You can change anything once you accept — acceptance gives you a place to start. Relinquishing control of things you never could control to begin with allows you to focus on yourself. Is there something you can change in yourSelf to make it easier to cope with the present situation? When we change ourSelves, things change around us! Whether you stay together or not, allow the answer to come your way from a state of empowerment. Make choices on what you will not accept; this is done by feeling inner peace first. This is the only effective way to lead a life that reflects you inside and out.

When the energy is pulling away, you recognize that some of the reasons have to do with you and some do not. Your vibe, your frequency, your state of being all attract responses in other people that match you. So, you go back to working on yourSelf full-time while that person hopefully works out whatever they need to work on and comes back around. Sometimes there was nothing there to begin with, sometimes it was all a trip in your own trickster mind. Look for the good in every moment, including the moments that make you feel sad — then don't be sad.

Go back to enjoying the parts of yourSelf that make you feel proud of who you are. If the person comes back, welcome them from your good place — and if they leave, both results can be beautiful.

Did you allow your emotional wellbeing to rest within the palms of a stranger?

Don't close the book on the relationship completely, there's a reason this person came into your field and you started liking them. There's no need to make rash conclusions. While you go out and enjoy the forest and the trees, leave a little spot for them to come back. And when and if they do come back, smile knowing they would have done so all along if they wanted to. And, once again, you choose if this is what you want. You always have a choice to opt out or keep going.

Finding meaning and purpose in life and becoming our own best friend first is what gives us peace. Working on ourselves. Building those building blocks. Transforming our energy and kneading the knots out of our restless minds.

Breathing out loud a few times throughout the day helps a lot. Take a deep breath and breathe out loud with a big sigh, like an animal in the forest. It's fulfilling.

There is nothing we can do to bring someone towards us who, for whatever reason or psychological impasse outside of our control, does not want to make a step in our direction. Lest we forget, we have the same ability to choose.

Have faith that you have been your best with no regrets, and release that trust into the Universe. The Universe is a vast and generous place for the taking. Believe in what is in store for you and expect it to attract the right outcomes. If you're not meant to have what you have now, trust that there is something even better for you just around the corner. Because there always is, love wants love to win.

Not Feeling Worthy

> *Insecurity is the worst sense that lovers feel: sometimes the most humdrum desireless marriage seems better. Insecurity twists meanings and poisons trust.*
> **GRAHAM GREENE**

Don't. You are always worthy.

Self-worth goes back to self-love and acceptance of reality.

You are worthy. You were born into this world, you have a body, and you are alive. You are worthy of every single thing that every single person has in this world! Even if you don't have it yet, you are worthy of having it, okay?

Now, even though we know we're worthy, we might have to rely on other parts of ourselves to hold ourselves up. Be the suspenders of whatever situation you're in with whatever you've got inside that helps you recognize your greatness.

And, of course, read this two or three times: You are worthy of finding and being with your match, just as much as anyone else. You are worthy of moments that feel like predestined, manifested magic. You are worthy of a relationship that makes you feel unconditionally safe to self-express without your vulnerabilities being used against you. You are worthy of exactly what you want.

Before questioning yourself further, decide if this person is truly who you want and whether their insecurities are triggering yours.

Your immensity and power and magnificence must be felt by you at the core of your being when you're with that other person.

When we put our worth in the hands of another person, we lose the keys to our house; in a sense, we are no longer in charge of its upkeep. The other person might not be able to put a finger on what's happening, but they will feel the pressure of having to maintain what's ours to maintain.

When we place our worth in their hands, they will notice our sense of Self getting watered down somewhere and aimlessly trickling into side streams with no clear direction as we wait for their approval to dictate where to go next.

You're not dating a tsunami. You can't let them decide every way things are going to go based on how you need them to make you feel about yourself! You must already make yourself feel that way. And by the way, a tsunami of their attention and love, no matter how overwhelming it feels, can destroy you alive, so decide if that's sustainable. Your ability to hold space, feel worthy and be seen by that person is either there or it is not. Part of any relationship is the deep emotional connection you feel with yourSelf — and the rest, well, you can't force it.

If you find that you are putting your own self-worth into the other person's image of you — whether that be through waiting to receive a text from them, choosing to dress a certain way, denying parts of yourSelf in conversation that the person might not be so keen to hear you expressing — just know that kind of energy must go somewhere. It is felt. Your Soul suffers when you do this, because it knows you are so worthy of being seen and expanded by being seen. So be real. Either way, you will learn the lesson, but being real will save you time.

If you feel like you can't handle the rush of emotions and maybe you even thought you were holding the reins at first, notice those little wounds inside you that have subtly taken away your control of the situation. And why was it ever about control to begin with?

Instead, ask yourself what made you suddenly lose your own grasp on self-worth. Did they pull away for their own reasons and yet trigger your assumption that their distance surely had to do with your value as a person? Did their absence spark the start of a dramatic film in your mind? Was your brain playing the impostor syndrome on you all by itself? Or were you mirroring a hidden insecurity from them? Or, or, or? There are so many reasons you could suddenly not feel worthy in a romantic relationship, but this fundamental symptom of low self-worth luckily all leads back to you! And you can change You better than you can change anyone else. As a matter of fact, that's our individual superpower and all we can do.

It can feel natural to want to sabotage a relationship when these feelings arise. Have you ever asked yourself if you're actually the one afraid of the commitment? Despite thinking it's what you want and what you are pursuing, are you indirectly and secretly craving the other person's hesitancy? In this case, perhaps because you do not feel worthy? Are you secretly falling into insecurity on subconscious-purpose?

Insecurity is pervasive. Once noticed, it should be transformed. It's a pandemic in the Universe of your mind. When you see insecurity in action, you must work on changing it into love for yourself.

Love your insecurities, love them as much as you love the greatest feature in yourSelf. Because it's through love that you will get out of the scariness of it.

Let's end this on a good note. Remember who you are. Who you were before this silly little hiccup came into your life. Who will you be in a few months when you get that job, do that presentation, kick ass on the field, beat your own records, or sit on the freaking beach like the *Quing* of your castle, owning your body. Because you're incredible. For real. Of course, it's nice when someone you find amazing also thinks you are amazing—it's like a double meta compliment. But love is love. It's a frequency, a field that surrounds you that you create and starts from you.

Love yourself and love will be all around you. That will always be enough.

You are so worthy of a situation that makes you feel good. Now go get yourself an ice cream, or a hot chocolate, or a vegan Thai dish, or a deep tissue massage, or a mani-pedi.

Love yourself. Love your journey. Love all of you.

CHAPTER 8

EARLY TOGETHERNESS

The love we give away is the only love we keep.
ELBERT HUBBARD

You may have thought this next section would finally be about daisies and roses and the start of a fairytale come true. Love your optimism, it looks good on you, keep it! Of course you feel this way right now!! Depending on where you are on the cynicism spectrum, right now everything is perfect. They can screw up your coffee order and you can forget your umbrella, and it's still a great day (as it always should be). However, it has been my personal observation that the beginning of being with someone can also open up a Pandora's box of emotions that need to be dealt with.

Once you are aware of certain demons, you need not worry because the awareness itself will neutralize their effect. So here we'll examine the demons that might come out of you or them (which is normal). We are also accounting for the possibility that the relationship won't make it (don't be attached to outcome!). As much as we might love love and the idea of making it past date three with someone who meets our criteria and shares our values as well as our ideas of the future, sometimes we miscalculate. Sometimes we are blind to something because we wanted for it to work so badly. Both people can have this disorder of putting companionship above compatibility and, dear goodness, good luck to them on their shaky raft at sea. Other times, by date fifteen the fuel to the fire ran out faster than we expected, a little thing became a big thing (like lip smacking, sports watching, day drinking, poor communication patterns, etc.), we learned new non-negotiables, and discovered we wanted to end things.

These moments are just as important as the positive aspects of new love, and when we can live through them with honesty, we make room for the good and pure love that we deserve. It's always okay to start over, and it's great when you've found your place to stay. Whether it is with or without that person, every experience brings us insight into the love we deserve. The more we are able to discern this and make brave and honest long-term choices, the more we keep ourselves free for our highest purpose.

So let's go through these steps together and I promise we will end on a good note.

PAST DEMONS CREEPING UP

> *What is required for many of us, paradoxical though it may sound, is the courage to tolerate happiness without self-sabotage.*
> **NATHANIEL BRANDEN**

New relationships can bring out all sorts of sour sides we didn't know existed. Our sour sides can be a surprise! We can unknowingly self-sabotage, basking in the fake love that everyone but us can see. We might anchor to our past, glorifying it, and putting the new person up on an unreachable pedestal. We can believe we are undeserving (see "Not Feeling Worthy" in Chapter 7).

All of these root causes that are unrelated to the person we are dating can manifest in completely strange ways in ourselves and in the other person. At that point the simple answer is to retreat to home base. Figure out what just happened—because a *whole* bunch of things can happen—and with the awareness mindset we've instilled so far you'll be able to catch yourself before you wreck yourself. If not, then bless you! You'll get yourself a whole new lesson to learn.

Are You Settling?

> *There is no passion to be found playing small—in settling for a life that is less than the one you are capable of living.*
> **NELSON MANDELA**

Be careful not to play the biggest joke on yourself.

Sometimes, we want something so badly and we want so much to believe that we've got it all figured out, that we will ignore every single clue that what we are doing is absolutely wrong for us long-term. One time I dated a guy and things were so perfect in the beginning (see "Love Bombing") that I wanted it to last forever. I was completely lying to myself—the relationship was blocked and impossible to move forward from. And you know what happened? I got a herniated disc. I was flat out on my back for weeks while friends politely asked me, "And what do you think this is telling you about your life? Your relationship?" I was at the peak of my spiritual learning and *still* I did not want to see the reality that was blatantly screaming at me.

I was, in fact, settling. I wanted to believe in the overall picture…but there were things about this person that were huge compromises for me! For example, he didn't believe in spirituality and thought my meditation practice was "cute." He didn't care to learn English or ever speak it with me, except for the phrase "I like high heels," and watching movies together meant never getting to hear Jason Mamoa's true voice because of dubbing. These were things I felt I couldn't settle on.

What is the danger of lying to ourselves to keep something going, or denying parts of ourselves in order to humor our fantasy? We filter and choose only the information and people that support our cause, and we become defensive when anyone tries to challenge, even in good spirit, our beliefs about what is taking place.

People who are under a spell of wanting something to work, no matter the cost, will not recognize the value of this topic until it has taken a toll on them. If you are experiencing playing a joke on yourself *right now* by settling for something that feels safe, I'll save my last pizza bagel for you and we can laugh together when it's done. I can assure you, we have all been there to some degree. I know you are well intentioned! But listen to what Rihanna says: "I always believed that when you follow your heart or your gut, when you really follow the things that feel great to you, you can never lose, because settling is the worst feeling in the world."

Take the person who chooses not to see the gaps in compatibility with their partner because all they want is to get married. It's similar to someone who chooses to study, train, and pursue a line of work purely because of salary and appearance.

Career decisions can be adjusted with relatively little collateral damage, but choosing your life partner is not a joke.

You live your life in your bubble, happy, whistling through your day, until suddenly you wake up and think, "Oh, no. This might be wrong. So, so wrong." It may be a small voice at first as a series of irrevocable decisions (such as engagement or talking about marriage) start to enter your field, and you realize the monumental backtracking that must be done in order to go back to point zero. But at least by going back to zero you would be authentic again.

Be very careful and very discerning when choosing your partner, before investing the rest of your life into them. It should be someone with whom you feel good and calm, and with whom you are able to live your life freely while sharing a vision of the future across all of your powerful dimensions. The sides of you you know about and the ones you will keep on discovering and strengthening throughout your life.

Do not be in such a rush to get what "you want" that you miss yourself and the importance of what you need in order to be authentic. By having the courage to face and refuse what isn't right for you, even at the eleventh hour, you will always come out stronger. But if you can prevent that, do it sooner. Trust that what you need is right around the corner—it's not about waiting forever for someone to come, it's about alignment, and energetic alignment can happen very quickly for you when you are ready for it.

Who cares if the situation you have gotten yourself into was based on honorable intentions—if we forget to use the heart inside that loves us first when choosing our partners, we've lost the battle of authenticity. No matter how fair, responsible, and objectively attractive the person may be.

Come squeaky clean with yourself, because you may have this tendency. Keep it between you and you, but ask yourself if you've done it or are doing it.

If you are the last one to find out what you already knew, you will know that while you were in that state, not even this book could have saved you. In any case, it is here for you should your Soul choose to wake from its slumber, and so is the last pizza bagel.

Memories from Previous Relationships

Sometimes I miss you, which is strange, because you weren't at all the way I remember you.
JACQUELINE SIMON GUNN

Most of us going through this journey will have at least one past relationship. A relationship that moved us, that withstood the test of time and perhaps patience, which became a point of comparison for the next one, or the one that hasn't happened yet. Buddhist wisdom tells us to live in the present, because when the past becomes the present, you lose the future.

Memories are funny little things, though. What do we do with these spells of the mind when they hit us?

We release them by acknowledging them, allowing them to pass through us in whatever state we are in. We can say things like, *I see you, memory! You're trying to come in. Come in, then. My door is open for a spot of tea. You are not my present, though. I have changed since I last experienced you. Thank you for showing me this old movie scene. Stay as long as you need. The bathroom is the second door to the right.*

Sometimes the memory could be coming up to warn you. Maybe you're dating an emotionally abusive person and the memory is there to show you not to fall for the initial red flags. This is what experience is for! Pay attention to it.

But what about when we self-sabotage with the past, using it as an escape from our current unhappiness and glorifying it to believe that what we have now is not as good?

A healthy memory should feel like that flavor of ice cream you used to get as a child. Sweet, distant, and not in any serious competition with the happiness of your current reality. Detached, yet reachable with a quick thought. You could go get yourself an ice cream right now and be differently satisfied without completely derailing your life choices.

The problem arises when we seek comfort in our past as a sort of excuse for what is lacking in our present.

Sentimentally speaking, this can be dangerous for the following reasons:

- It prevents us from fully shutting doors so that new ones can open properly.
- It blocks us from experiencing life in the moment (and growing).
- It sends the message to our subconscious that we are not able to control our present state of well-being.

How can we ever feel at peace if we are subconsciously telling ourselves that something that won't come back, that we *can't* get back, is the solution to our present moment?

Be careful with tapping into your memory to feed off of better days. Lower the volume of desire that accompanies that good memory. The impact of that memory shouldn't be proportional to your present reality. There is always something great to experience in your present if you are feeling great within. And if you are not feeling great within, then that's your emotion to wear now, not an old pair of heart-shaped lenses.

Let's say you've drifted into thinking of someone that, for whatever reason, things didn't work out with. And you think, *If only I could have those moments again, I wonder how I would live through them knowing what I know now. I would do anything to go back and see. I should have never quit that relationship.* You find yourself replaying those movies in your mind. How easily you would work things out now, how familiar that person's flaws are, how much you would trade to have those now rather than the ones you have.

When we play those movies in our minds, the air smells sweeter, the gazes are deeper, the attraction is palpable, and the problems don't seem so insurmountable.

But if we were to go back to taste that ice cream, maybe we'd find the flavors to be superficial — just like if we took a walk through our old high school hallways, things might seem smaller.

Acknowledge this, and tread carefully when you access memories. Do not hero-worship or romanticize the storytelling; it will take away from the bliss and the glory you can have today. Always speak well of them, though. Afterall, they are someone you once loved.

And if the glory and the romance you have today still doesn't seem to measure up? Let the relationship go, and enjoy your single voyage for just a bit longer.

ENDING A RELATIONSHIP

Nothing in the Universe can stop you from letting go and starting over.
GUY FINLEY

I'm going to do things a bit backwards and hopefully propel you into a positive mindset as you are about to read the next sections. I'm going to start with what it feels like to be alone for the first time in a while. Get used to this thought, it should not feel scary.

What is it called when you are able to intelligently go into a negotiation or agreement? Emotional leverage. Allow the idea of being okay alone to give you emotional leverage as you deliberate on your unique case of whether or not to break up now.

Being alone is strange because all of a sudden you notice it and sometimes you don't for extended periods of time. (Until finally, you just don't). It can feel unsettling and other times delightful. But to anyone who conquers the waves of emotion that trigger our well-being, being alone is liberating. Then it becomes normal again, once you develop a nice, steady relationship with yourself.

Start by getting comfortable with the things you most fear, such as going to the movies or to dinner alone. Throw yourself at them if you need to. At the same time, be wary of what brings you too much confidence, like over-drinking at the club while telling yourself you are doing you.

Just because we were once excellent at being alone, doesn't make us great at it again. We may have developed some sticky coping habits along the way and now we've forgotten how to remain balanced in the freedom of being alone. Humility is the key.

Humility will bring you back to yourSelf. As will nature. We will always be part of a Greater Plan. Sitting in nature with humility and soaking up that gentle power of pure existence in the trees and the mountains and the forest, not to mention the fresh air, and the Sun, will give graceful pauses to your disquietedness.

Sure, you may see couples walking by, looking like they have it all figured out — plans, children, and passionate embraces. Allow them to exist freely and peacefully. If they can do it, so will you! Your job is to enjoy being alone now. Being completely okay with it.

If you're at home, light a candle, and be in a clean, fresh environment. And see if the following chapters on whether to break up apply to you.

Ending a New Relationship

Change is hard at first, messy in the middle and gorgeous at the end.
ROBIN SHARMA

Relationships work when they work. They flow. Particularly in the beginning, they feel great and bring lots of joy to both people. It's simple. Both want to please one another, yet are able to remain grounded in their own energies and time. No one is giving more than the other; partners are in sync and compatible. In a perfect scenario, both are giving without counting, and so much love is being shared that no one knows which direction that love is coming from.

A relationship can start well, with open, forthcoming, and caring communication. There is laughter, compatibility, and seemingly aligned values, but things can still take a turn and go wrong. People change and evolve, or more likely they begin to show more of themselves.

When there is a block in the evolution of a relationship—even between two well-intentioned people—and new, triggered sides emerge, those new sides are hard to unfeel and unsee.

If you reach a point where you feel you are keeping score of who is giving what, or saying what and when to the other, then you could be at that point. When the enthusiasm—or the desire to make the other person smile or feel good—has gone missing, that is a bad sign.

Chemistry is the first to go, though it doesn't ever have to leave. It depends on the couple's effort to nourish their relationship flame. Sex can become the *only* thing keeping you together.

It takes two hands to clap, and both people have to want to be watching the show. Here are four questions to ask yourself when you're unsure of the current dynamic with your partner:

- When you feel as though you are making excuses to convince yourself that things are still going well, that's when you need to ask yourself the tough question: *Is this sustainable?*

- When you find you've made an effort to fit into the other person's image of an ideal relationship with you—because subtly, perhaps not even on purpose, you've noticed what they like and now you are doing it—ask yourself, *Is this serving me? Where have I GONE?*

- When you are made to feel as though you are too needy, ask yourself, *Are my needs less valid than theirs?*

- When you settle for less than you imagined because you think it's all you can get, ask yourself, *Am I better off alone?*

And when you decide that you might be better off alone, set that peaceful boundary. Do it with courage. Do it with finality. Because either you truly need to reset your needs and balance your expectations of someone else, or this particular relationship has managed to wreck your ecosystem and you must restore it. Prepare for the right person who will come your way next.

Someone always will. For every door that closes (properly), another door opens. Be sure to close the door properly. Without anger. Without fear. Accepting that this relationship is not right for you. Welcome the unknown, and free yourself from the purgatory you feel stuck in.

You deserve to be cherished and appreciated, to make someone feel as if they have won the lottery to be with you. You, too, are worthy of giving that gift back and making someone beam with joy because they want to receive it from you. It's beautiful to give your open heart to someone, but only to a person who will cherish it and be able to give their heart in return.

Ending a Long-Term Relationship

> *How do you know when it's over? Maybe when you feel more in love with your memories than with the person standing in front of you.*
> **GUNNAR ARDELIUS**

Every story is unique, and every relationship has its individual reasons for ending. It is hard to generalize about this particular aspect, so what I offer here is an anecdote from which you may be able to detract subjective meaning.

In a long-term relationship, the beginning of the end tends to creep up on you. You'll have withstood *so much* together for years, the thing you least expect is what one day breaks you. Up until this point, you had always come out of tough spots stronger — or at least your mind goes to the moments you had. Better yet, you had learned how to make the conscious decision to come out of challenging situations and still be together. Time after time, this creates a compounded value. The familiarity of the amicable partnership you've grown to share over the years is the glue that holds you together behind the attraction (if you have it still).

That amicable partnership feels so warm and fuzzy, doesn't it? Maybe you live together, and you can't imagine what you would do without the couch or the cat you raised together — or maybe you have a six season, twenty-four episode Netflix series to finish watching, a friend's wedding coming up, deadlines that keep you going passively into the future. Overall you get along — perhaps even better than some of your friends, it seems — so maybe life isn't so bad, right?

As I said, it creeps up on you. You find yourself doing innocent research. Googling things like "Signs my relationship isn't working out" or "When he says he needs space" or "Dealbreakers in a LTR, Reasons couples break up, How important is sex in a marriage when everything else is amazing?" You even add the word "amazing," like you're trying to reassure yourself and the search bot.

And you read and you read, falling into a series of internet rabbit holes. Judging other people's stories, thinking you don't have it so bad…Picking apart your own story in your head…*Well! They don't do that. Maybe we're fine. This is ridiculous, people do that?*…or *Oh, wow, it's kind of uncanny how similar I feel to this — could it be? No, it really can't be — I mean, it's just an article.* So then you tweak the algorithm to find an article that validates you more. But you still remember what the previous article said—maybe you even paraphrase some of its points in the next argument, or "strategic conversation," you have with your partner, as academic validation for how you're feeling. And in the middle of these conversations there are baptisms and birthday dinners and shared hiking trips with couples you've known forever, and things seem to be okay as long as you are distracting yourselves.

Yet something in your mind knows better than you do. Your heart knows all along what your mind can't yet admit.

You wrestle with it in your head: Is this settling or is this just mature love? Is this what it means to reach the five-, ten-, fifteen-year mark? How can anyone truly know?

You do. Your heart knows. And only you can make the decision. It's the decision that makes you feel lighter when you think ahead. It's the decision where you love yourself more after it's done one year from now. It's the choice that comes from your inner Knowing.

It takes courage, it takes honesty, and change is never easy. Particularly when there are years of trying and lots of people around believing in your love. But remember that in this life only you can know what you need and how you want to feel. Just because the relationship ended it does not mean it failed—for all the time you were together, it succeeded. Not every journey is forever—forever is a long time.

TOXIC RELATIONSHIPS

Toxic people attach themselves like cinder blocks tied to your ankles, and then invite you for a swim in their poisoned waters.
JOHN MARK GREEN

Sleepless nights, blaming, spinning wheels in your brain until you have no idea who started what fight with whom, who is right, who is hurt (everyone). And between every second you are thinking of ending it, you remain intoxicated enough to keep going back. Or you question your decision to end it in favor of making it work, even though that's as probable as a herd of monkeys with keyboards writing the Divine Comedy.

Sometimes a perfectly nice and unsuspecting, well-intentioned person will attract someone unhealthy into their lives. It appears random and out of the blue, but there is no such thing as a coincidence.

You could be progressing quite well on your personal growth path when such a person comes along to test whether you have learned what to walk away from. Or maybe you consciously chose to expose yourself to the situation because you were intrigued by what you didn't know and felt a certain pull to explore that further.

When relationships turn toxic, it happens rather quickly. Meeting that person might have initially given you a quick sense of familiarity (this is your trauma recognizing the exact same future trauma about to be played out). You might have felt like you had known them your whole life, so it was very easy to cross into a blurry-lined sense of security. For whatever reason (be it spiritual, psychological, sexual), they are calling you to acknowledge the pain of something you have not yet healed from, so it feels natural to quickly become close and openly fight.

The whole familiar dynamic becomes inevitably alluring and develops in an insidious way. At first, like a drug, it's incredible to be around them. You can't stop learning about each other and sharing all your deepest secrets. Narcissists and some other personality types will then use this information against you later, but it is more complicated than that and we will touch on this soon.

The important thing to take from this section is to learn to feel your instincts in order to prevent this situation from happening, remain centered if the situation has already started, love yourself more so that you can get out of it, and love yourself *even more* so that you can recover from it.

We will not be elaborating on physical abuse, although toxic relationships and dynamics are often, unfortunately, precursors for this. I would like to emphasize a zero tolerance policy on this and hope you will too.

Toxic Dynamics

> *The most painful thing is losing yourself in the process of loving someone too much and forgetting that you are special too.*
> **ERNEST HEMINGWAY**

Toxic dynamics start off rather innocently, otherwise we would never fall for the trap to begin with. The person usually disregards boundaries, so they may call or text you often — things you wouldn't necessarily find alarming since they can also be signs of a promising and secure relationship.

Remember, when a relationship works, it just works. That's a simple phrase to keep in mind.

A toxic dynamic *is* a dynamic where two people fuel the frustrating predicament together. Whether *you*, the receiver of the abuse, like it or not, you are opting into the toxicity. It's the equivalent of willingly throwing yourself into the burning flames of a house that would never have caught fire had the person you're trying to save not lit the match. There's an expression that goes like this: Stop setting yourself on fire to keep someone else warm.

Here are some signs to look out for in yourself if this type of dynamic gets created:

- **Self-care begins to take the back seat**; whatever self-care means to you, you suddenly justify canceling your important appointments or self-commitments in order to accommodate the other person's needs. You start ignoring your own needs.

- **Losing touch with others** because this person takes up so much of your time, both energetically and physically. You may find yourself slowly putting your healthier, less demanding relationships on the backburner. Eventually this can turn into isolation.

- **Jealous and controlling behavior starts cropping up**, including gaslighting, unreasonable suspicion and mistrust from the other person that completely erodes the relationship.

- **Walking on eggshells** and being at the beck and call of their moods, fearing that anything you do will trigger a negative response. Walking on eggshells leads to the next warning sign.

- **Losing yourself and your ambition**; you start forgetting what it feels like to think for yourself, only doing things according to what you believe will make the other person feel good or remain "calm." This leads to forgetting your own opinions, even in simple matters such as deciding what you want to eat or wear.

- **Receiving the blame** for circumstances that have nothing to do with you. These circumstances are created and escalated out of nowhere by the other person. It can feel like they are twisting the truth so that no matter what it is you've done, it was "wrong."

If you're exhausted reading this, I am exhausted writing this. This dynamic is crazy-making, and whatever you do is never enough. When two healthy and happy people meet, they are already complete and they add to each other. Neither of the two should feel as if they are carrying the other, as much as it can seem alluring.

Our minds like to know we're right about something, and we blame ourselves to compensate and protect the image of the person we want them to be. This projection can escalate very quickly into covering up worse things down the line.

Be aware early on when something feels off. The 'off' feelings are micro-signs that could indicate you're headed in the direction of the above signs. You might feel it in your gut at first — perhaps getting into fights that make no sense, barely recognizing yourself at times — and you may feel as though half of you wants to break up and half of you could never detach, like the shell of an oyster.

Listen to your inner knowing.

Some people won't love you no matter what you do. Some people won't stop loving you no matter what you do. Go where the love is.
KAREN SALMANSOHN

When you notice someone does something toxic the first time, don't wait for the second time before you address it or cut them off.
SHAHIDA ARABI

The most judgmental people are often those who complain most about being judged. The ones not complaining will look as though they're the ones doing the judging.
CRISS JAMI

Controllers, abusers, and manipulative people don't question themselves. They don't ask themselves if the problem is them…they always say the problem is someone else.
DARLENE QUIMET

7 things negative people will do to you. They will…
1. Demean your value;
2. Destroy your image
3. Drive you crazy!
4. Dispose your dreams!
5. Discredit your imagination!
6. Deframe your abilities and
7. Disbelieve your opinions!
ISRAELMORE AYIVOR

What happens in a Toxic Dynamic?

In a toxic dynamic, one and eventually both people shift into an unhealthy loop of needing each other to feel fulfilled. One is the taker and the other is the giver. Eventually, it becomes so chaotic and jumbled, nobody knows up from down or who caused what. The giver is always seeking to justify the behavior of the taker, minimizing the bad ("If only I ignore this part, the rest is wonderful!"). The toxic person, the taker, is also a master at pulling the right strings when they sense they are losing control over their partner, and will know how to manipulate the right moments.

The giver clings to the early moments where things felt fantastic and keeps the hope alive that everything will soon settle back to "normal." *They just need to see that I am not going anywhere, that I am a good person, that I will not hurt them the way others have*, etc. They make excuses for their partners in order to account for their difficult past or shortcomings. Of course, for the person instigating the toxic dynamic, there is no turning back. They are receiving exactly what they want: validation that they are worthy of being chosen by a good person, glimpses of what it feels like to have a stable mind, but most of all, someone to share their suffering with. Ultimately, a toxic dynamic comes down to their great suffering, which needs to be exposed and then healed.

Do I believe toxic people are hopeless and evil? I do not. We all can change — this is the beauty of life! But it takes a lot of self-awareness and determination. And while a person is unaware that they are the ones exacerbating their own pain with their own suffering, it is impossible to reason with them, let alone date them. Never accept such an arrangement. If you are in one now, start imagining ways to be with someone who adds to your life and wants to make you happy.

Dating a person who is unhappy, insecure, and toxic requires the other partner to be willing to compromise themselves continuously and buy into their misguided way of seeing things.

A toxic person has certainly never been able to feel inner peace, so they have never been able to access their true Self. The only way for anyone to have a chance is to heal themselves first. Truly heal, as in learning what it feels like to love oneself. I'm no doctor, but I'd say this kind of healing takes at least six good nights of ayahuasca, two peyote ceremonies, and a mushroom microdosing regimen. In order to complete this journey, one needs to lose their sense of self that is triggered by external validation, which is in their Ego, and start rebuilding themselves.

A person who has attracted and survived a toxic relationship will need to heal themselves, too. Deeply. To understand what it was inside of them that did not sound the alarm and instead made them run into the arms of that toxic person. How did they allow themselves to make choice after choice that would break their own spirit? What made them put someone else's pain above their own? Which parts inside of them were they looking to heal through this relationship?

There are many, many questions to answer in our healing journeys. But the final solution is always the same: Love.

We look at what happened, we acknowledge that it happened and why. This neutralizes it. Then, we don't forget it but we let it go, and we move into Love.

This is why it is so important to learn what it feels like to be loved by yourSelf. It allows you to learn to hear and defend your own voice, the one that wants the best for you, the instinct of when to book it and when to stay. Learn to make difficult choices in the short term in favor of paving a beautiful path for a future that is rewarding and easy for you.

Everyone has a right to be respected and treated fairly by the person they are dating.

Love yourself first, then share it with those around you.

Good Communication

Words are the voice of the heart.
CONFUCIUS

Let's cleanse our palates from toxicity and focus on the positive, so that we can work towards attracting that instead!

Communication is unique to every relationship you have, and particularly with romantic relationships it's up to you to decide whether or not something clicks well with you. One of the biggest mistakes you can make is to cut someone off because of some way you think they've offended you, when in fact you are not offended at all.

For example, if you were to communicate with someone who writes to you every three or four days and it bums you out not to hear from them more, well, you let them know! However, if it doesn't bother you so much because you know you will see them and when you are together you feel safe, heard, and understood, then what bothers someone else won't be an issue for you.

What does healthy communication look like?

It's transparent, not manipulative.

It's direct, not passive-aggressive.

It's trusting, not suspicious.

It focuses on the positive and neutral, and seeks to alleviate the negative.

It comes from, and assumes that it will be met with, good intention.

It allows room for disagreement.

It seeks resolution, not blame.

It is loving and kind, not judgmental.

It is respectful of boundaries and time.

It is open and non-expectant.

It is energizing, healing, or pleasant.

It encourages growth and enlightenment.

It gives room for all participants to take the stage when they need it.

It leaves space for humor.

It flows.

It's safe and secure.

Much of the above occurs when each party in the relationship feels motivated and invited to level up as someone from a positive place, with no hidden agendas or repressed emotional suffering. And it is awesome! You can have a little healing and suffering, because everyone is always growing and working on themselves — but the key is to be aware of it, own it, and not make it the other person's problem.

Being able to laugh, express yourself, grow, and trust in a loving, direct, and reciprocal way is a surefire ticket to success in any relationship. When the conversation holds good intention, anything can be said, and it will be received with the same energy. Different people will bring out different sides of you, just don't forget who you are. Go with the flow of your energy and their energy. It is said that when two people are in a relationship, it is a relationship between them and a third energy, which is their uniquely created and shared experience that evolves from their communication over time.

Enjoy learning new sides of yourself from the mirrors of others!

Do it benevolently, unsuspiciously, and with an open mind. You never know who is right for you — it could be someone completely different than you ever suspected.

Breaking the Toxic Cycle

> *There comes a time to stop trying to make things right with people that won't own their part in what went wrong.*
> **UNKNOWN**

Right, let's get back to it so we can close the cycle. When toxic relationships end, it's seldom a clean break unless the toxic person wants to leave first. In which case it might be a narcissistic thing, where they stop getting what they needed from you, drop you like a hot potato, and go on to their next feeding.

What you want to do, figuratively, is bulletproof yourself in a padded room to make sure you won't be pulled back into the cycle with them — which you might be, let's face it, many times…until you learn.

What's important is to expedite any lingering desire to explore the dynamic (all the more inadvisable if there have been physical altercations), leave the situation for as long as is necessary, gather up your stories, and start sharing them with others for perspective.

My least healthy relationship was in my mid-twenties and it fully altered my sense of self, diet, and interests during that six-month time frame. It ended in a very intense way when I felt physically threatened during a long night when our normal, non-stop arguing turned into something unusual and I had to call the police. He didn't touch me directly, but he did pour cold water on me in my sleep to wake me for more arguing just before shattering the glass bottle against my wall and keeping me awake until 4am, which sabotaged a very important day I had the following morning.

I was so utterly confused, but grateful to have watched enough Lifetime movies to know that abusers send you flowers after they've abused you. Which he did, a couple of days later.

How did I ensure I didn't go back? I told everyone what happened to make sure they would hold me accountable for not going back. I also booked a six-week package with a therapist who talked me through the logic of what had happened to me.

Flowers, emails, and attempted meetings did not work on me. I was done. It did take a lot of time to get the solicitations to end.

> *Forgiveness is a personal process that doesn't depend on us having direct contact with the people who have hurt us.*
> **SHARON SALZBERG**

Then, I forgave him. I told him the only way I could do so was if he let me go. And he finally did.

It's important to take note that there are varying degrees of toxicity, there's a difference between someone who drives us mad with intense energy day in and day out, and someone who is acting like a bit of a player in a hot and cold scenario. The former may be more pressing to cut off, the latter could just be a sexy problem you continue to chase until you recognize you need a bit more self-respect.

The goal is to break the cycle, or recognize you will have to eventually, then realize it is bad for you and a resolution will not be possible as long as that person remains stuck in their current script.

You will feel confused, dizzy — almost like getting off the spinning teacups at Disneyland — so seek validation from external benevolent sources. Lean on your loved ones so you can get the strength to change what needs to change in order to feel, know, and live in the space of self-sufficiency. Now.

It's not easy in many cases, but it is worth it.

> *The question is not whether you are doing good or bad. The question is that you are there.*
> **OSHO**

The only growth we can control is when we change ourselves. And perhaps it's no coincidence that something worthwhile comes down to feeling worthy. Remember it, defend it, promote it. You find worthiness within, by understanding and owning that you had a hand in saying yes to what just happened, not judging yourself for it. It was what it was, a new lesson to learn. Moving forward it will not happen again, you have learned to love yourself more now. Congratulations on getting here.

CHAPTER 9

PARTNERSHIP

With a little bit of inspiration from the Universe, mixed with past experience, my current experience of being single, and the helpful guidance of some of the happiest and longest-married couples I know, I have compiled this next section.

WELCOME TO LEVEL II

The most important thing in life is to learn how to give out love, and to let it come in.
MORRIE SCHWARTZ

Leveling up is scary. Until it isn't. But for many of us who haven't entered this space in a while because we've been focusing on self-improvement (in order to one day be ready for this very chapter!) it can feel that way. A true relationship, where both people are giving it an honest shot, can be scary. It can feel like you don't have any idea what you are doing, and it can be overwhelming.

Imagine closing off all of your options for the unforeseeable future (if not forever) for someone. And now, imagine them doing it for you. Because they want to. Because they actually like you enough to do this with you. All these things can happen gradually or automatically, it doesn't matter—but at some point these conscious decisions are being taken on both sides.

Not one relationship is the same, though similar milestones and trajectories exist.

Letting go and allowing the emotions to rush in without feeling any type of way about them is a daunting task, but what is the alternative? Remain single and safe with your takeout and Netflix? Indeed, that's not to be underestimated, but this next part is for the brave Souls that choose to embark on a path of Love with another person.

This is my stance on what *real* love feels like. You are welcome to take anything you wish from it into your story.

If you are lucky to be found by love, it is a mirror, just like any relationship you choose. When love enters, it feels unavoidable. It fills you with the beauty your partner sees in you, in themselves from being with you, and in the surrounding world. It's knowing you are adored for being exactly who you are, your mind and your values—which is why in order to be able to receive it, you have to love yourself first. Real love makes you feel capable of doing anything you want, being anyone you want to be, with the unconditional and equally invigorating support of someone cheering you on as you do the same for them.

Love is giving space so a person can be themselves in their own expression. Allowing them to take up space next to you, instead of overwhelming them with yours. It's trusting and it's benefit-of-the-doubting because something solid, something you can feel inside lets you know you can trust this person.

Real love comes once you've learned how to give it to yourself. This feeling of real love feels extra special to someone who has experienced healing from not having loved themselves.

Krishnamurti states this similarly in reference to total self-abandonment.

Total abandonment can only happen with the understanding of oneself, Self knowledge is the beginning of wisdom, and therefore wisdom and love go together. Which means there is love only where I have really understood myself, and therefore in myself there is no fragmentation at all. Which means no sense of anger, ambition, greed, separate activity.
KRISHNAMURTI

Love is the freedom to walk your own mountain while your lover walks their own. Other times it's walking together. Nothing is separate, they are one of the same. It's that confidence that you are both working to be your highest selves, and beyond any circumstance, the certainty you will respect the choice of one another over all else. This is the binding principle which sets the foundation. You are together as a team yet individual in exploration—you are in loving complicity. You are equally responsible for the well-being of the relationship, knowing that choices made together or apart have an impact. And you do so easily, without pressure, because you love each other calmly and it is not a question.

When you have the freedom to explore your curiosities and ambitions individually, you come back to one another with novelty and growth. This is what fuels and keeps the relationship alive. It's what keeps LIFE—and therefore your lives together—alive no matter what.

You create your reality together, fostering an environment where feeling satisfied with oneself is celebrated—life is not meant for suffering!

Expect reminders from your partner in order to stay on track, and let them know when they aren't being at their best. Honesty in action.

It is beyond the monetary, but it's also a business relationship with financial duties. When your spending habits align, it's easy for your lives to match up to co-create. When you are open about finances, as uncomfortable as it might be, the love will become enlarged by making conscious choices to support this.

Respect is sexy. So is gratitude. Remain true to yourself and defend the right of your partner to do the same. Knowing someone will always have your back brings strength, confidence, and courage. Celebrate the successes often and with happiness for each other whenever one or both of you achieved something great.

Remain humble and know that everything you have is a blessing.

It's looking into your partner's eyes and feeling your Souls recognize one another for a split instance that lasts an infinity. It's a feeling of paradise when you're together. It's sensing their heart's goodness matching the warmth you feel in yours. This lifetime, you have chosen each other, and you've also chosen each other above all others to trust with business and family and health and…insert your own unique story here!

Love creates excitement to conquer a situation, an objective, and life itself. It's encouraging. It's that little side smile in the middle of dinner that only you understand—it's the glow in their eyes when they talk about you to your friends.

It takes a lot of internal work to be ready for love—some stumble upon it and work through it together, others work very hard to break through their patterns to get there. Whoever you are at whatever stage in your life, have faith you will find it and it will find you.

Challenge and Surrender

> *Think not you can direct the course of love, for love, if it finds you worthy, directs your course. Love has no other desire but to fulfill itself.*
> **KAHLIL GIBRAN**

When it hits you, love is like the wind propelling your sailboat forward. It is the whisper of the ocean breeze on your cheeks, and feeling so completely yourself that you are intoxicated by it. And yet, as you stare in awe gazing at the stars, your feet are firmly planted on the ground.

You remain on your pillars as much as you can, because you cannot control Love when it happens to you. You surrender to its teachings and trust you are prepared and worthy of them.

Your match is, of course, going to greatly improve your life—but they will also challenge you, as you will challenge them. It is by challenging one another to be better that you remain at a good level of attraction, not to mention good people. At the same time, you accept what comes to the table openly as you create a space of safety for self-expression and self-realization.

It's nice to have a degree of stability, while also welcoming spontaneity. Safe doesn't necessarily mean boring. A table is stable, but it can still have a modern, sleek design. Look good and treat each other well, for yourselves, and for each other. It's a safety net you build together. That person isn't yours to keep, they are there of their own free will and so are you. It's wondrous to recognize each day that you've chosen each other and not take it for granted for one second. Go back to this perspective from time to time and your bedroom hours will stay exciting!

We remain at a good level of attraction when both challenging one another to be better, while at the same time accepting the delicious meal each brings to the table. Actively surrendering and trusting at the same time.

Challenging is not to be seen in a negative way or something to bring satisfaction at the expense of the other person. It can actually be harder to challenge someone than it is to allow things to remain at status quo. The status quo is comfortable, predictable. The status quo is sex on the third date—challenging is seeing if they'd be willing to wait a little bit to get to know you.

Lazy days together in your slippers and drinking a nice glass of merlot in the evenings is swell. But if every weekend is lazy slipper day and every evening is merlot night, then this is where one person must have the strength to challenge the other to push beyond their perceived limits of potential. If this feels like an issue to them, then we have the right to choose how we want our lives to look and how to respond to everything, and when we enter into a partnership, we owe it to ourselves and to the other person to continue being the best version we can be. Never stop pulling your own weight.

Surrendering is the complement—it means not resisting. Releasing control. Receiving. Allowing things to flow in the way they should go and not sitting there thinking who will do what for who, and what is the righteous thing to do in a particular instance.

When we surrender, we trust. We trust the other person to guide us in times we might be spiraling, we trust them to know the difference between when we are having a bad day and when we need to change our act.

Most of all, we surrender to the feeling of love. To its magnitude. One of the hardest things to do is to just surrender, allow things to flow through step-by-step, without drifting into imaginary scenarios. Always sit in the present with the knowledge that reality will come and it will be just right. It's the things we can't control that teach us the importance of surrendering. And people, including our partners, are things we cannot control. Once we let go of control while in a state of personal growth, we surrender to the rest, and we open ourselves up to the most incredibly rewarding and growing journey we can take with another person. A love journey!

Jealousy

> *It is not love that is blind, but jealousy.*
> **LAWRENCE DURRELL**

Jealousy can be insidious. This trickster may appear at any phase of your romantic journey with someone, so let's get into it!

Like any emotion, jealousy sprouts from within as a reaction to certain external triggers. If something triggers a jealous process in us, it's because that thing contains the perfect ingredients to bring our cocktail of triggers to life. These underlying wounds are begging to be seen and healed. We can address our jealousy and rid ourselves of it at once, or we can choose not to address a given situation, blame our partner, and invite plenty more occasions to turn up until we learn the jealousy came from us.

We can be irrationally jealous because we feel like we are not enough. That one is on us. We are always enough. The easiest way to mitigate this, of course, is to find a partner who loves us unconditionally, shares our values of trust, and sees us completely for who we are. In order to attract that, though, we must be that for ourSelves too.

Yet, we could still find ourselves feeling jealous of a particular person that shows up in the periphery of our relationship, and when this happens we should stop and do an objective assessment of that person.

Is there something they have that I do not have? And is that something that I *could* have if I wanted to, or is it a complete left turn from my identity?

In the first example, say that person is a yoga instructor whose body is in really great shape. Have you been taking care of yourself lately? Eating right? Exercising? If so, perhaps you are not jealous of that person *per se*, but rather of what they represent—something you haven't been providing yourself. Recognizing this will help you to see it is not about them. It is about *you*. And you can fix it.

In the second instance, perhaps that person is a blonde and you have dark hair, or they are a different race than you, or a completely different body type, or ten years younger. Are you sensing a total exasperation inside because you'll never be able to be them? Rejoice! Surrender into the fact you are nothing like them. Your partner chose you. Resist feeling hopeless and rest in knowing that your partner chose *you*. There is nothing you can do but be your truest shining Self.

And if for some reason this inkling does not go away, in the eventuality that some situation were to occur, isn't it better to recognize this development from a place of confidence? To notice that, in fact, you and your partner were not right for each other? This perspective is liberating as well, because it means a better fit for you is out there too. Release the situation with love.

Let's indulge in another potential scenario of jealousy. Let's say we feel jealous because, on some level within us, we sense the insecurities of our partner, therefore we sense they are ripe for receiving external confirmation from others. This is a bit of a vulnerable recipe that, mixed with attraction, can result in mistakes being made. But we cannot change the level of confidence in our partners, not in the sustainable way that they could if they were to give it to themselves.

In a long-term relationship, we are playing the long game. The goal of the game is to stay in the game (if we can call it that), to perpetuate the game that matters to *us*. When we give up on winning or losing because we just want to keep dancing, we stop feeling jealousy.

Envy is okay. We can wish we had someone else's physique for a hot second, or their knowledge in a subject matter—but we mustn't get caught up in it. We mustn't get caught in the notion of coming in first place or second place. Loving ourSelves is about rising above that duality and recognizing we are the complete package. If someone has certain qualities that exceed ours, great! That is always going to happen. There will always be someone smarter or better looking or more fit, or younger, or older—but are they you? Are they your complete package? No!

Be confident in that. And share what you are feeling with your partner. Give them a chance to change your mind about what you are thinking. They may not have realized that their behavior was easily misinterpreted and, moving forward, they will be more mindful. You might be surprised to learn that much of this dynamic you're jealous of was coming from you. Then, like any challenge in a relationship, talking over the situation brought you closer and made you both more capable of understanding each other.

And if indeed this issue was the straw that broke the camel's back, gather the pieces from lessons learned. When we choose a partner, or any relationship with another person, we either get love or we get a lesson. Or we might even get both. But if we do not try, we get neither.

Blissful Balance

> *Your hand opens and closes, opens and closes. If it were always a fist or always stretched open, you would be paralysed. Your deepest presence is in every small contracting and expanding, the two as beautifully balanced and coordinated as birds' wings.*
>
> **JELALUDDIN RUMI**

Imagine you are floating on a river with your love, carried by its smooth water, the Sun is kissing your skin, and tender, refreshing splashes are gliding by the bottoms of your feet as you remark to yourself how blessed you are and what a beautiful day it is to be alive.

And you're light and free, you've completed all your days' work and your future obligations have reached a plateau of repose, as you blissfully embrace *la joie de ne rien faire*.

Together you feel unstoppable—how could anyone come near the bulletproof shield you've built around one another's affections? The flowers bloom for you, the children smile, and even the bugs don't stay too long on your legs.

The river is gentle as you follow its flow and you need not do anything to enjoy it fully. This is a beautiful gift from life to pause in gratitude. But you must not forget to remain active in this ride—perhaps the water will soon change and require you to navigate away from the rapid streams that may be approaching. In this way, you keep one eye open to the bliss and one eye open to adjusting along the way.

Relationships are alive, they are a creation of you and your partner and just like any other living thing, they require nurturing and attention. Learn to identify early when it is time to adjust for unsteady waters so you can balance out the current and maintain a steady flow. And when the river is flowing easily, take the time to relish in the wonder of your journey together.

I thought about what to call this section for some time. Bliss was the easy part. We can all relate to this feeling, even if fleeting—we know bliss well. We experience moments of bliss in all sorts of relationship contexts. It's our right to claim it if we want to make the best of life together, but what is the counterpart of Bliss within a healthy relationship? It's certainly not agony—that would be a highly volatile structure which I have no interest in exploring. So, the counterpart is Balance.

Balance is when you recalibrate, you do whatever it is you need to do to fill up your cup so that you can continue to bring back the luscious nectar your relationship needs that is unique to you.

Bliss can only be achieved through Balance. An awakened consciousness will not allow for anything less, and if we are not achieving balance or wholeness through our own interests—meditation, music, food, friends, and work creations—then we are taking too much from ourselves in order for the relationship to survive. Like when we stop eating, our organs start to eat themselves. Don't be energetically anorexic. Feed yourself fully, become satiated, and then watch the cup overflow together.

> *Love gives naught but itself and takes naught but from itself.*
> *Love possesses not nor would it be possessed;*
> *For love is sufficient unto love.*
> **KAHLIL GIBRAN**

It's similar to when you are just dating, where there are times you sense you need to get a bit of your energy back. Do not ignore the calling to go back to yourself and into yourself from time to time, especially in a committed relationship. No person should be dependent on another's person's happiness—we are all responsible for bringing ourselves back to our center.

This is what we trained for, right? We got all the way to the end of this journey ready to live a big life, one where we accept all outcomes as long as we are clear-minded in pursuit of our path towards greater awakening to fulfill our purpose. And when we find someone who matches these desires to live life in this big way, we must not be afraid when the moment to trust one another and to seek balance comes along, whether separately or together. Because when you do come back together, it will be *even better* every time. When both partners understand this and can do this as frequently as when they notice the tides getting stronger, then you will ensure growth and smooth sailing for the life of your relationship.

No one will feel threatened or abandoned, because over the years you will have learned that this flow happens naturally between you both.

COMMITTED PARTNERSHIP

I saw that you were perfect, and so I loved you. Then I saw that you were not perfect and I loved you even more.
ANGELITA LIM

They say the best partnerships are those where each person looks at the other and feels as though they've won the lottery. I'll take that with a side of chocolate cake, please.

But, more realistically, I was thinking about what embarking on a solid relationship feels like to me. Suddenly, my mind takes me to a casino where I'm putting all my chips on the table for a game I've never played.

I do know one thing. Rather than seeking people who need help, it's best to find someone perfectly capable of driving down their own road so you can climb your own mountains. You'll be beside each other all the while, just in different ways.

Space to Thrive

The greatest gift you can give someone is the space to be his or herself, without the threat of you leaving.
ANONYMOUS

It's tempting to want to be attached 24/7 to the person you love and cherish, and it's a great sign if you feel this way. But if, for whatever reason, you need to be apart, you should also feel calm and confident about being on your own. Beyond this, you should feel motivated and excited, because life is always motivating and exciting!

When two people merge together without forgetting who they are in the first place, they leave room for each other to continue growing in and outside the relationship and this gives them both space to thrive.

Space to thrive physically creates room for you to fulfill tasks and passions that fall outside of the relationship and help you remain grounded in yourself. Space can be anything from having a girls' or guys' night or weekend out, to pursuing unique hobbies or doing your thing whenever you need to.

Space to thrive mentally entails allowing someone to assert themselves without criticism (either direct or indirect) and not interfering in their authentic self-expression. This lightness and freedom in communication dynamic leaves room for your relationship to expand.

Love is a choice. Even in the most committed, legally binding scenarios involving asset sharing, love is still a choice. You should feel free to stay and free to leave. Of course, you will not want to leave something you've built together if it is giving you joy and space to thrive, but in order to create joy and space to thrive you must provide the space to choose.

There are times you are completely in sync and times you are just a bit over their bullshit, and that is where you will be challenged.

Unconditionally

> *Unconditional love really exists in each of us. It is part of our deep inner being. It is not so much an active emotion as a state of being.*
> **RAM DASS**

The key takeaway here and always, is that until we can give it to ourselves, we cannot sustainably receive it from others. Only *we* can reliably fill our tanks, so if we love ourselves unconditionally, then it becomes easy to love everything unconditionally, including our partners!

Unconditional love doesn't mean loving everything about the person. It means not needing them to be different than they are for us to be happy and accept them. It's when we are wholeheartedly okay with another person being who they are without asking for anything to change. Attraction is like looking through a diamond on one side and finding only that side beautiful—unconditional love is seeing the whole diamond and even its imperfections.

Of course, if the person changes in appearance or, goodness forbid, something happens to them, two people will hopefully still be there for each other unconditionally.

We are complex, imperfect human beings, who are in constant cyclical evolution of healing and growing and clearing and receiving. Infinite circumstances and consequences surround us and can push us to become people we never thought we could become. We could spiral into a rage one day, or sadness or depression or anxiety. Of course, we try our best not to, and when we achieve a certain threshold of inner peace and an awareness of our own energy, this happens rarely—how*ever*, it can. And should you lose your sanity for a moment, you want to feel safe—without hurting the other person—that you won't lose the one person you need for support. When you are feeling like the world is crashing down on you, the last thing you need is someone to make you feel worse for it. So! You should feel safe in your crazy and safe in your healthy.

The opposite of unconditional love is criticism.

It's a real shame in a partnership when one has a challenging day at work (e.g. not having said the right thing, saying something silly at the wrong time, etc.) only to receive a double critique from their partner that contributes to the negative self-talk on how one should have behaved differently, or acted smarter, or known what to say in the moment. This makes us feel twice as bad and extremely ineffective at life. It won't make us stronger, it makes us insecure in ourselves and in the relationship.

Unconditional love provides one with a safe space to be human and make mistakes, it's a warm set of arms to greet you after a long day. It's when you are seen for who you are, for the beauty of your Soul behind the masks of societal illusions. It's your buddy standing beside you, right there, in life. For better or worse. Unconditionally. Reminding you of your strength.

Being Whole Together

> *The purpose of a relationship is not to have another who might complete you, but to have another with whom you might share your completeness.*
> **NEALE DONALD WALSCH**

The real secret to being happy in a way that spans across your relationship is to be whole all by yourself. Oftentimes people will ask me why I am still single and I've mistakenly said, *"Because I love being alone!"* But this is not the full response. The full response is: "I choose being alone over being with someone for the sake of completing me, since I already feel complete. But I would love to meet someone who feels the same way."

A synthesized conversation between two people who feel whole looks like this:

> **Partner A:** This is how I see the world, and it works really well! I do things this way and I am happy.
>
> **Partner B:** And this is how *I* see the world, and it works so well for me too!

Then you both trust each other to go on living your lives in this mindset. And when one of you needs support from the other, it's like this:

> **Partner A:** This situation has come up…and I am doing this about it, but I am not sure.
>
> **Partner B:** That's a tough one. In my world, I would do it like this…if it helps to hear a new perspective.
>
> **Partner A:** Wow! I'd never thought of it like this, thank you! That's actually very helpful.

When this happens, both partners know they have themselves and each other, and this makes things ultra-abundant. Completing someone is good for Hollywood, but life wants you to complete yourself. It's about compatibility rather than completion. Cookies go well with milk, but they also can stand alone and mix with other foods.

Being whole also allows you to feel less jealous or tempted to seek in someone else, what your partner may or may not have, because you already see it in yourself.

When you feel whole and good about who you are, even if sometimes you notice yourself slipping into a lesser mindset, you will know a few important things:

- What it feels like to be there

- That it's time to work on it again

- How to go back there

- That only you can do it for yourself, otherwise it wouldn't be yours to claim.

It's not a matter of creating your wholeness, it's a matter of digging it out. It was always there—we are born whole. So the strategy is not so much to pile more things onto yourself, but rather to remove. Remove, remove, and remove the layers until you can revel in the simplicity of who you are. The well doesn't dry up—we have merely lost the way to reach its waters.

Each time we find our way back, we see that it was in us all along. How nutritious our own medicine is so that we may continue to be active partners in the dance of giving and receiving wholly in the relationship. Sometimes it takes a bit of time to do the work and understand how to regain footing.

Once again, we can appreciate the cycles that happen in life and the cycles that happen in our partners' lives. Life is not linear, it is cyclical, so we mustn't beat ourselves up when we notice we have fallen out of alignment with the full power of who we are and what we can give ourselves (which is everything). It is by accepting every shadow aspect of ourselves, that we do not ask our partners to complete us.

CONCLUSION

MARRIAGE

Give your hearts, but not into each other's keeping.
For only the hand of Life can contain your hearts.
And stand together yet not too near together:
For the pillars of the temple stand apart,
And the oak tree and the cypress grow
not in each other's shadow.

KAHLIL GIBRAN

I'm married.

Just kidding! I am enjoying privately dating someone. Or not, depending on when you are reading this. There is absolutely no rush in what it becomes.

Point being, I can't talk about marriage right now. I am about as qualified to talk about marriage as I am to comment on the Winter Fencing Olympics.

Who would I be to comment on marriage? I could compile a research report, citing references and other people's opinions, but that wouldn't be anything of unique value and I certainly would not be able to personally validate any of it.

I started this book during my very own personal crisis. My crisis was an accumulation of a lifetime of externally driven misunderstandings that seemed to happen *to* me and not *for* me. One fine and crazy day, with no place to escape to, no space to run, I found myself facing my inner demons for the first time in a loving way.

Step by step, meditation after meditation, I began to understand what it meant to enjoy carving out time for myself. It was like opening the blinds slowly; at first I could only see the immediate benefit during that one hour in the day. Eventually, I would feel that benefit for a greater part of the day. Now, I feel and can call upon the sunshine inside me all day long. Most days. I'm still normal, and some days can still be trying.

But overall, we could say I found a love for mySelf so powerful it radiates towards all those around me. When in this state, my love for others is so big that it has healed my family line, my general friendship line, my ability to set peaceful boundaries, and my desire to share this love with all those around me.

Just because these lessons and insights came to me in this order does not mean they will follow that same order for you. My first realization could be your last, and my last could be your first. Time is a construct; we are not bound by such nonsense beyond this dimension.

I hope you feel a sense of calm and peace from reading this. Now is your chance to become your own elevated and illuminated *New Banana*.

Never get used to beauty, including your own. Continue to marvel over its magnificence.

Thank you for being on this journey.

To learn more about Holy Shiver and our upcoming projects, including meditations, events and future book releases, scan here:

Printed in Great Britain
by Amazon